AFRICAN HISTORY

EXPLORING THE AMAZING TIMELINE OF THE WORLD'S RICHEST CONTINENT – THE HISTORY, CULTURE, FOLKLORE, MYTHOLOGY & MORE OF AFRICA

HISTORY BROUGHT ALIVE

FREE BONUS FROM HBA: EBOOK BUNDLE

Greetings!

First of all, thank you for reading our books. As fellow passionate readers of History and Mythology, we aim to create the very best books for our readers.

Now, we invite you to join our VIP list. As a welcome gift, we offer the History & Mythology Ebook Bundle below for free. Plus you can be the first to receive new books and exclusives! <u>Remember it's 100% free to join.</u>

Simply scan the QR code to join.

Keep up to date with us on:

YouTube: History Brought Alive

Facebook: History Brought Alive

www.historybroughtalive.com

CONTENTS

INTRODUCTION

In 1000 B.C.E, a San man lowered himself behind the bushes, turning his head quickly to his brother as he muttered a soft series of clicks. His hands gestured toward an Eland Cow grazing in the field afar, alone and unprotected. The brother replied, and a plan was formed between them. They hopped off to opposite sides of the field, prepared to chase the cow with the wind so that it wouldn't sense the danger waiting (Balyage, 2000).

The men got into position, and a voice chanted the opening of the hunt.

The brother raced out. His cries scared the cow, and it fled. An arrow zoomed through the air, and a sudden thud raged through the quiet morning as it pierced the beast's chest.

The San man sent up a silent thank you to Kaggan, the great God, for he himself must have enabled them to find such a feast. The meat would never be finished among the members of his own family, but perhaps his neighbors and their families would enjoy the sentiment; after all, were it not for their relatives in the east, they may not have eaten at all last month.

Every part of the beast would be used. If it couldn't be eaten, they would find a use for it. The hide would be turned into leather robes, and the bladder used to transport water.

He looked down at the ostrich egg strapped to his waist.

The hole on the edge suggested that its time had come to be used by his first wife in her jewelry making.

His eyes darted ahead, his brother's chants of thanks distracted him from his thoughts.

He started off toward him.

Suddenly, his pace was interrupted by the sound of angry, vengeful words he could not fully understand. However, the tone and few similarities in dialect were enough for him to have recognized that these people believed him and his brother to be thieves.

He moved quickly to try to stop the argument starting between his brother and the strangers, but he was not fast enough.

He felt the wind beat into him, knocking his breath out as his brother fell to the ground, a blow dealt to his head.

What he and his family would not uncover for thousands of years was that the people who took revenge on his brother were the long-lost children of two starstruck lovers. The first partner belonged to his own tribe, and the second to a great enemy. Little did the tribes know, they had both come from one parent.

How was it that twins would become enemies and birth children who would ultimately destroy them?

African History tells the most exquisite tales of woe and wonder. They are the breathtaking originals of stories you may recognize from your textbooks on Ancient Egypt, Rome, and Greece. Ancient Africa is where it all started. As the birthplace of the human species, it's only natural that Africa also gave rise to many of our languages, philosophies, myths, and legends.

History Brought Alive breaks into the most recent and unknown historical research around African history, to create a uniquely sincere and detailed timeline of events.

Using reliable resources managed by credible researchers, eyewitnesses, and aural keepers, History Brought Alive tells a true drama that will have you curling your toes in awe and anticipation.

While many texts are outdated, History Brought Alive uses recent material and new scientific evidence to solve mysteries that have been questioned for decades.

Great time and empathy have been put into providing an accurate telling of events. While many historical accounts can be seen as disjointed, History Brought Alive strives to provide a coherent and believable flow of events.

History Brought Alive writes from the perspective of the people of Africa in an attempt to protect and preserve history as they know it to be. For who would know it better?

This book relays a detailed account of how Ancient Africa was developed, starting with its very first inhabitants. The book takes on the difficult task of piecing together the pathways taken by *Homo sapiens* and in doing so, presents one of the most fully structured current presentations of Ancient Africa. The book encapsulates the newest findings by world-renowned archeologists into an exciting and riveting time capsule that will leave you feeling as though you are watching from over the shoulders of the first Bantu speakers as you journey with them through their migratory patterns, cry over their losses and marvel at the Kingdoms formed in their victories.

This book will change the way you view Ancient Africa.

Every account you know, every story you have ever been told, is only half the truth.

Ancient Africa might just be the greatest land ever known.

CHAPTER 1
HOMO SAPIENS IN AFRICA

In 1925, a black man working in a mine in Buxton, South Africa, wiped the hot sweat from his head. He shivered, his body reacting to the lime chemicals he had been submerged in for weeks (Tietz, 2018).

He stretched out his hands, and leaning his shovel in between his legs, he clapped away the dust that had resided on his fingers, painting them whiter than he had ever remembered seeing them before.

His wife would complain if she saw him like this and tell him to wash the grit out from his nails.

He would have if he had expected that he would catch less dirt on them.

Wondering for a moment if he and his daughter were

alright back home at his village, he pulled his shoulders back and smacked his shovel back into the dirt, kicking the spade in deeper. Leaning into the handle, he reaped the earth from its grave.

His eyes grew wide and his chest tightened as the face of a small child stared back at him...

Perhaps showing this to the management might afford him a raise large enough to see his family over the weekend for the first time in months.

The Tuang child handed over to Raymond Dart became the first form of scientific evidence that humans were derived from apelike ancestors.

After the discovery, a series of diverging bone fragments were uncovered in the area now known as The Cradle of Humankind, the place our ancestors are believed to have congregated.

Africa was an abundant paradise of streams and animals and an agreeable climate in comparison to some of the harsher and colder landscapes of the time. Africa was the perfect place for creatures to explore and live. Africa, during Pangaea, was a place considered now to be, the Eden from the Bible.

These creatures grew, the stronger and wiser individuals being the last to survive during such intense times, governed by ever-present carnivores and environmental disturbances. These stronger and reasonably more intelligent individuals banded together and, over time, evolved to create a new species of hominid. The last of human ancestors is understood to be *Homo sapiens*, though, with today's research in genetics, it's not uncommon to hear of people having partial Neanderthal genes.

Despite the coalition of genetic makeup, the first evolutionary groups reported are the San and the Hadza who are believed to have lived approximately 20,000 years ago.

What happened to the rest?

There must have been so many Homo sapiens in Africa, how could there only be two groups that were documented?

Africa has a rich and fascinating history that is difficult to translate into a set timeline. Exactly how, when, and where the groups recognized in society today came to be, we may never know. But the most common consensus is that *Homo sapiens,* who emerged approximately 200,000 years ago, evolved in Africa from *Homo erectus*, who emerged approximately 2 million years ago and then were struck by a heated change in the environment (Penn, 2019).

Where the land was once dry and pliable, it became soft, wet, and watery. *Homo erectus* tried to escape the clutches of their submerged environment but perished.

It is believed that *Homo sapiens* and Neanderthals lost their ancestors' more peaceful nature thanks to the growth of their prefrontal cortexes, which heightened their cognition and made these newly evolved species more territorial and aggressive than those before them.

The last of *Homo erectus* was believed to have been found in the north of Africa, submerged in the aftermath of an earth collapse.

Homo erectus never made it out and became extinct one hundred thousand years ago.

Neanderthals and *Homo sapiens* never felt the need to migrate beyond Java. They were smarter, more organized, and more structured in their planning than *Homo erectus*. Their new, wet environment suited them fine.

Despite the similarities in their biology, *Homo sapiens* had a larger prefrontal cortex, making them more intelligent and violent than the Neanderthals.

Though the groups could presumably live in harmony as long as they remained out of one another's way, *Homo sapiens* possessed one significant ability beyond the rest that ultimately led to the fall of their companions. *Homo sapiens* possessed the ability to communicate with other groups. Neanderthals could only communicate about resources and things. Neanderthals understood family through memory and instinct; their amygdala and emotional processing sectors in their brains were large, but not large enough to lead them to destroy the *Homo sapiens* before they themselves were destroyed.

Homo sapiens conducted trade and gossip long before they evolved into the people we know and see today.

Language was mainly a series of dialects understood by most *Homo sapiens groups* within close proximity.

This ability allowed them to talk about feeling threatened, ridiculed, or distasteful of the Neanderthals.

They captured, killed, fed off, and enslaved their ancestral sibling into extinction.

Soon after the fall of the Neanderthals, approximately 40,000 years ago, the land quaked, Pangaea began to separate further, and the environment mirrored its new location (McKie, 2009). Heat, unlike *Homo sapiens,* had ever known before, crept through the paradise they had once called home. Most of them left, moving eastward through Europe and toward Australia, curiosity, and dreams of an easier way of life pushing them on. The groups split after leaving Africa, chasing resources toward the places they would settle into and become what we know today.

Two significant groups stayed behind, growing and evolving into the first reported descendants of *Homo sapiens*. These were the Hadza and the San people. Both groups drifted through Africa, following the flow of resources. Both were hunter-gatherers at the time and would settle wherever their needs would take them.

CHAPTER 2
THE SAN

The San and the Hadza, after thousands of years drifting through Africa, separate and unaware of each other's existence, found themselves meeting once again at the Great Lake around twenty thousand years ago. The Hadza preferred to find themselves along the north of the lake, while the San preferred the Southern parts. Though the two had originated from the same source, they found from time to time kinship in but one regard, their language.

The San and the Hadza communicated using a series of clicks, chatters, flicks of the tongue, and other explosions of the mouth and throat.

This was a complex language, where mouth position, click intensity and even tone were pivotal in communicating succinctly and meaningfully. Much like in any language, the San used verbs, nouns, adverbs, prepositions, and context when communicating, making their language one of the first complicated forms of language to be spoken.

Groups and Political Systems

The San people were originally hunter-gatherers, having no need for growing crops or raising livestock. These nomads would move wherever their resources would lead them. There was no hierarchical system and no one person who ruled them all. Instead, immediate families grouped together in a band, and each member had equal say over the handling of issues and concerns. The bands, however, would each have a designated chief who would be held with the challenging responsibility of monitoring the usage of resources. The chief was by no means more important than the other members, nor could their opinions override those of opposing parties. Their sole purpose was to account for the resources collected. This individual was usually the eldest and most respected member of that band and could be male or female.

Bands would group themselves through loose family ties and general residency to alleviate the challenges of everyday living. As a larger group, the San would participate in a variety of projects together. On each project, there was a respected chief, not one who led them within the project, but one who had a particular affinity for it. Children, women, and non-San descendants could still be viewed as individuals with great knowledge that should be heard and taken into consideration in the greater group discussions.

One of the projects that they were engaged in was hunting, which was predominantly handled by the men, but women could participate too. Another was the gathering of seeds, berries, and plant-based foods. This task was mainly done by women, but men were allowed to participate. Throughout the tasks the San engaged in, there is little regard for gender differences, but rather, the bands focused on gender capability. Other tasks included healing, cooking, inventing, crafting, and teaching.

For the most part, the bands would live separately in their own caves and housing formations. When there were celebrations, marriage proposals, rituals, or battles, the bands would move in closer together. While each band spoke its own dialect of the ancient San language, they could also understand the dialects of the other bands.

As far back as can be traced, it has been found that the San lived in Southern Africa, mostly congregating around the Western Cape Coast, though it was not unheard of for the bands to stray further north.

Spiritual Beliefs

The San believed that there existed a Greater God, Kaggan, the cunning hero and trickster of creatures who created everything from the mountains on the horizon to the fish swimming through the stream. He is the creator of miracles, fortune, luck, rain, and glory. He could appear as anything, even an animal, though his favorite animal was believed to be the eland cow (which is actually an antelope).

In the beginning, Kaggan created darkness, which was called Ga. There were no stars, no moon, and no fields. Ga married a beacon of light who would soothe his clouds and bring light to the day. They moved to a quiet cave where they birthed three daughters, the Mountains, the Plains, and the Waters. Their three daughters loved to go outside the cave and dance. Their parents liked to watch them, as did Kaggan. One day, Kaggan appeared to them in the form of an antelope. Seeing the Antelope, the girls and their parents captured it and cut it into five pieces.

While they carried the meat home, Water, who held the head, noticed the eyes twitching.

"Why have you hurt me so?" the head said, staring at her. The girl screamed and tried to explain what she had seen to her family, but they all thought she was imagining things, after all, she had a habit of being a tad dramatic.

The head began to vibrate, and so did the other parts. Water screamed and screamed until her family complied and put the pieces down. The pieces cracked and creaked before flying back together. The skin stitched back up, and the bones straightened. Once complete, the Antelope rose and looked at the people who had butchered it.

Since that day, man would forever know the God that is Kaggan and be humbled by his power.

The people who had a greater understanding and connection with Kaggan were the healers. Healers were not particularly gifted individuals with a spiritual conquest or who had experienced an awakening of some sort; rather, the San preferred to have many healers. Anyone could become a healer, but the process involved many days of travel and much sacrifice. It was not easy. The healers, once anointed, would indulge in visions or patterns of thinking in which they would encounter psychic instances of illness or death in battle or accidents, even when the participant involved was hundreds of miles away.

Following their visions, the healers would host trance dances where they would attempt to see further, and/or heal the rest of the group. The healers would dance, stomping their feet and clapping their hands to a beat as they twirled around in the landscape they called home. The other members would sing and chant, and when ready, would join in. Their trance dances would last anywhere from an hour to several hours, often resulting in slight seizures or episodes. Once started in one individual, the seizures would begin to travel from person to person, healing the individuals who participated and allowing the healers to restore both mental and physical health in the group and see the context of their strife.

If you happened to stroll upon such a sensitive and private occasion, your heart might begin to beat rapidly in time with the rhythms, and your body might sweat as you stared into the glazed eyes of the locals, healing their own through the passion of entertainment and spirit.

Along with Kaggan, they recognized his godly brother, Kagara. Kagara was evil and cold, and he was often found to consort with the dead. He brought disease, famine, drought, and pain among the living as he conspired with the souls of the dead to bring the living down into the darkness with them.

The dead were a jealous and hateful group. They weren't forgiving and kind, even if they had been in life.

The San were so afraid of the dead that should a family member or friend pass, the band would move, never to set foot over the area again. They believed that the souls of the dead remained there, independent and easily offended. Walking over a known grave was a feared task taken on only by those outside the clan.

Most San buried their dead and marked the grave. Even if a band didn't know the soul that had passed, they would have to be richly tempted before they would dare insult them by disturbing their rest.

Interestingly, although the San feared the dead, they did not fear death, nor did they harbor resentment for it. It was not uncommon for a mother to birth a child in the coldest of winter when resources were limited and force the breath to leave the baby before burying it shortly after birth. That isn't to say that they didn't grieve their losses but rather, that those losses were expected.

The same applied to new life. There was little festivity over the birth of a child and often pregnant mothers, along with a significant other, would retreat into a private space to birth the child before returning and reuniting with the family. There was no spectacle, baby shower, or large celebration.

The San often spoke about their acceptance of the inevitability of life and death, weaving these philosophies into their artwork and storytelling.

Folktales

The Musical Child

One such story told around the campfire went as follows:

Once, there was a Lynx, whose beauty was beyond comparison. As a child, alone and stranded, she met the Anteater. The Anteater's heart melted upon meeting the beautiful, sweet child and decided to take her and raise the Lynx as her own since the Lynx had not a soul in the world.

As the Lynx grew, the Anteater became aware that her child's beauty caused much stir among the other creatures. She gifted the Lynx a small guitar so that the threats surrounding her babe would become too distracted by the music she played to revel in her beauty.

The Lynx played every day at daybreak and every night at the sunset. Her song became the alarm for many in the area, including her mother, the Anteater.

One night, the Anteater noticed a rumbling in the earth, but thought nothing of it, for who would be so rude as to ignore her child's song while it played?

She went to sleep to the sound of her child's music.

A sudden sharp twang of her child's guitar stirred her in the night.

"Why do you play your guitar now?" she asked the Lynx.

"It wasn't me," the Lynx replied.

"How then could your Guitar play?"

"Perhaps it was a stick that had fallen," the Lynx suggested, for the two lived burrowed underground, and it was not uncommon for the earth to shift around them when there were travelers.

With her mind settled, the Anteater fell back asleep.

While she slept, humans came and stole the Lynx from her home.

When the Anteater woke and realized her child had gone, she quickly ran to the place where her baby had been asleep.

She felt the ground and noticed how soft it was. The ground was supposed to be hard. If the ground was soft, that meant that there was an air pocket somewhere.

She lay very still and felt the ground quiver with the

footsteps of the people who had taken her child.

The air pocket was connected to the surface on which they walked. If she were to break into the air pocket and then the ground below, she could break the surface on which the people walked.

Using her large claws, she dug deep into the ground.

Sure enough, the unsuspecting victims fell into a deep hole in the earth, and the Anteater raced to collect her child.

Upon her arrival, the Anteater told her babe, "Did you not know that anyone who took you from me would crumble into the earth and die?"

This story showcases the love a mother has for her child as well as the intrinsic adoration the San people held toward children, even those who were not their own. The San loved children, and even as adults, tried to keep the childlike wonder of life in their mind's eye (Lewis-Williams, 2018).

The Springbuck's Daughter

Another such tale uses the same characters but places them under different circumstances.

One day, the Anteater goes out and steals the Springbuck's daughter, to raise and love as her own. She takes the child to her underground camp, feeds, and cleans her.

The child's father finds out what has happened through

the words of a gossiping partridge and sends his valued ally, the Lynx, to bring her home.

While the Anteater was out hunting, the Lynx stole the child back and returned her safely back to the arms of her father.

But the Lynx also knew of the Anteaters' powers in controlling the earth and returned to her camp and waited for her to return.

When the Anteater came home and found the child missing, she went to the spot where the child had laid and searched for the open air pockets.

Before she could deal the blow that would send the surface of the child's home crumbling, the Lynx came up behind her and hit her over the head with a club, killing her.

The change of personalities within the characters is evident in San's belief that Kaggan can be and come in many forms. It further divulges the San's love for children, while also warning that theft, jealousy, and revenge are not tolerated (Lewis-Williams, 2018).

In the case of such incidents involving these spiritual ailments, the healers would perform a trance dance to cleanse the group and release the harboring of such negativity, which was believed to bring illness and danger.

The Lightning Fight

This story begins with a young woman on her wedding

day. After the ceremony, she returns to her husband's home, where she will spend the rest of her days with his family. She finds her husband to be unkind and finds comfort in escaping in her few moments of peace to be with her family. Her brother, unnerved by the hateful actions of his sister's husband, comes to rescue her and goads her husband into a fight. Perhaps it might have been an ordinary fight if both men hadn't been healers. The brother slams his fist into the husband's nose. Bleeding, the husband slams his hand into the ground, forcing lightning to shoot out at the brother from the sky. Dazed, the brother reaches behind him and, with the heat stirring inside him, flicks lightning back at the husband through the palm of his hand. Both men have been struck, and both have been wounded to the point of retreat. The husband went back to his camp, and with no one who loved him enough to tend to his wounds, he died. The sister and brother returned home, where their family healed them with herbs (Lewis-Williams, 2018).

This tale explores San's ideology of equality, that one who harms another may suffer repercussions. It also explores their belief in the supernatural as well as their need and appreciation for healers in their community.

Life, Habits, and Friends

The San were peaceful people without much greed or understanding of it. They lived their lives as they could, using whatever resources they came across. Where there was game to hunt, they would hunt it. Where there was grass to craft a bed, they would. The world was their oyster. This incredible gift of being able to master the Earth as they came to it, would also be their greatest downfall.

Before the arrival and creation of hybrid groups such as the Bantu, the Pygmies, and the Khoi, the San and their brother tribe, the Hazda, lived peacefully, opposite one another at the Great Lake. Both groups were hunter-gatherers and so would stray every so often from their humble locations, venturing out to witness what more their African continent had to offer. The San enjoyed migrating southward, while the brother tribe saw something more favorable lying to the north. Other sites aside, both groups had a place in Africa that they valued above all else, and for the San, that would be the territory of the Western Cape.

Given that Southern Africa was never particularly filled with fresh streams and lakes, it's no wonder that the San found comfort by the cape. Even today, the cape holds the freshest and most abundant forms of resources in the whole of Southern Africa. The San too, much like the modern locals, enjoyed the indigenous flora and fauna at the coast, hunting the brave antelope late into the night and stalking out the leopard before it stalked them.

To the San, the cape was home amongst many. All this would change upon their meeting with the new migrants—the Bantu.

The Bantu had a different way of life—one that none of the local tribes in Africa had experienced before. They were pastoralists, not hunters. They grew their own crops and protected their cattle with the utmost security. For the Bantu, their prized and protected game was spiritual. To the San, the land and the creatures on it belonged to no one, even if the presence of certain organisms, stemmed from the arrival of other parties. The San did not believe in income or valuables. They believed in survival above all else and, therefore, harbored and protected nothing other than their own people.

These differences in ideologies very quickly caused a spark to ignite between the two groups that would lead to plenty of battles and disagreements.

Though the feud between these two groups would remain lethal for years, the arguments were not without reward. As with any form of hatred, new conflicts are bound to arise somewhere—and they did.

The living circumstances between the San, their brother tribe, the Hadza, and the Bantu lead to the creation of various hybrid groups. The Pygmies, the Khoi, and varying merged Bantu tribes were some of the most well-documented groups to arise during this time of expanding civilization.

There must have been more, but, history does not account for the specific names of the groups that existed within these boundaries at this time. Though one can try and trace back the origins of languages in an attempt to pinpoint the specificities of the groups that lived at the Great Lake, it is by far a desperate attempt because of the amount of intermingling that occurred. There are so many similarities between the ancient African languages, and, these similarities can easily be identified in Indian and Asian languages as well. The contexts that they were created in are too lengthy and complex to present one language at one point in time. It's an impossible task, even in such a technologically advanced era as we live in now. Perhaps one day we will have those names and those intricate details, but for now, all anyone can account for are the broader ideologies.

Let it be understood before we navigate further through the ages and towards our current day and age that the Bantu were a collective group of peoples who spoke Afro-Asiatic languages. Among the Bantu were probably hundreds, if not thousands, of different groups of different skin colors, ideologies, and habits. Some of these groups already knew how to mine gold, while others had great relationships with dogs and horses. Some were the finest hunters the world had ever seen, and others had spent generations learning about and tracking the stars.

CHAPTER 3
THE HADZA

The Hadza, like many ancient African tribes, enjoyed storytelling. One such story tells of their beginnings. What's chilling is that the story reflects what scientists have confirmed today with regard to human evolution.

The story goes that there were once hairy, apelike creatures that roamed the earth called "The Ancient Ones." These creatures would hunt, kill and feed on animals without fire. Fire was not possible because of the earth's primitive state. There simply weren't enough tools to start one.

"After breathing in the blood of his feast, he would find a comfortable spot under a tree. He didn't sleep in a house because his environment didn't call for one. What good would a home do? What would be more comfortable than his spot right here?"

Years passed, and the Ancient Ones grew to become "The Intermediate Ones." The creatures were not as big as their predecessors and had no hair on their bodies. They could control fire and use it to cook food, warm their homes, and scare predators.

'The group had begun to notice how the animals avoided them. The animals didn't trust and lean toward the people as before. Instead, the animals raised their heads up, gathering in their surroundings, and once sensing a presence, would stalk the humans or run in the opposite direction. The group needed something to hide their smell, something that was as fast as the animals themselves. Dogs were seized and groomed to join them on hunts. They made for fine companions and bloodthirsty killers.

Finally, the group evolved into how we see them in relation to ancient Africa and their presence at the Great Lake. The "Recent Days" people had mastered the art of fire and lived their lives comfortably as hunter-gatherers. Their homes were reformed to cater to their belongings and special mementos. They had learned to craft containers for food, medicine, and beer. They had found solitude in their structure of living, working, and fending for themselves during the day while telling stories and gambling at night.

They had become inventors of note, laughing at the tradeoffs of close and foolish friends as they gave their belongings after having lost a bet. The rage of the loss never built for longer than 24, as the evening meal was always sure to alleviate such complications. They were never short on meat, for they had invented a precise bow technique and a deadly poison that they applied to the tip of their arrows. No beast would ever run too far from their plates again.

The Hadza of Ancient Africa grew beyond this scope to become the people that we know today, but how they did is more intrinsically remembered after their migration. It is from the years before that there is much myth and legend about them and their way of life, especially since much of the San had become under threat in the years leading up to the present day. Unlike the San, the Hadza hardly fell under the control of passersby (Madenge, 2021).

Groups and Political Systems

The Hadza didn't have a structured system, but rather, each person had an equal vote within their immediate family when it came to making decisions. They rarely interacted with their neighbors but might meet for entertainment purposes, gossip, storytelling, eating, and dancing. They didn't celebrate marriages, funerals, birthdays, or engagements but did celebrate the coming of age for boys and girls.

The men predominantly hunted, and the women gathered, though it was not uncommon for the roles to be switched. When the landscape was dry and animals scarce, the men would forage alone, sometimes bringing back small animals they were able to hunt while out. In the months when the resources were more plentiful, the men would travel in pairs and spend many nights tracking games before returning home with a large bounty of meat.

When a boy completed his first successful hunt and brought back a meal of extensive size, he was considered a man.

Women would often forage in groups and were almost always accompanied by a man. They carried with them tools to start fires, sticks to accumulate honey and dig for roots, and baskets for berries and shrubs.

The Hadza were resourceful people and their diet would change greatly depending on the season, their location, and their members.

Governed by where they might find their next meal, the Hadza moved frequently, and as such, did not have many belongings. In the hot summer months, when rain was limited and vegetation scarce, they would not build homes but rather camp on the warm ground and move daily in search of food.

Where conflict arose between neighbors, one would simply move further away.

Life among the Hadza was primitive and challenging. The locals were often exposed to diseases, famine, and malnutrition. Very few children lived beyond the age of 15. When a person or child died, they may have been buried or left for the landscape to consume. The kin of the deceased would then leave that spot, never to return again.

Spiritual Beliefs

The Hadza followed no religion but considered themselves to be spiritual beings, and they believed in two greater beings. These beings were the Sun Goddess, who created the earth and all its creatures, and her husband, Haine, the God of the Moon.

The men celebrated the God of the Moon through a special ritual performed once a month on dark nights. The men danced in the darkness, calling on the ghosts of their ancestors. They reveled in the history and tales of the men who stood before them, depicting their victories and sacrifices.

The ritual, known as the Epeme dance, was believed to build kinship between the men and bring good hunting for the months to come.

The Goddess was equally celebrated during the day through general blessings and greetings among friends and families. Her name, Ishoko, was embedded in many phrases, and her creativity, patience, and loyalty are told in countless tales.

Folktales

The Giants

There are many folk tales about Ishoko and her creations.

One tells the story of a Giant who helped her husband, Haine. Haine gave the Giant endless control over the

Hadza people as a gift to show his appreciation. But the Giant was cruel and unreasonable, forcing the Hadza people to work late into the night and eat foods that they didn't like. The Hadza people rebelled and moved away so that he could not control them. Angered, the Giant sent lions, previously known to be calm and peaceful creatures, to kill and eat all those that had ignored him. Again, the Hadza rebelled, fighting the carnivores that lunged at them. Still, it wasn't enough, and the Hadza had to seek help from neighboring tribes. In the dead of the night when the Giant could not see them, they formed a plan to trick him, and while his back was turned, they would shoot him with poisoned arrows. Their plan worked and, the people went back to living their lives free of restraints and orders.

However, it would seem that the Giant had not lived alone. He had brothers, and though his brothers had not the power to control the people as he had, they had the capacity for revenge.

Thus, a war began between the people and the Giants. The Giants were strong and large and could kill a man with just a flick of the wrist. But they were outnumbered and plagued by the same needs as their enemies. They, too, needed to sleep and eat and bathe. One night, once the two giants had gone to sleep, the Hadza and their neighbors came and killed them. Relief was once again restored among the tribe.

The Man-Eaters

Some of the Giants had found pleasure in feasting on the flesh of the Hadza people. Devastated that her creation had taken such a vile and evil turn, Ishoko appeared to the group of cannibals as a friendly snake. The Giants, not hungered by the appearance, as their favorite meal was to be found elsewhere, had no need to chase her from their home. While they slept, she bit them, and her venom sucked the flesh from their bones.

Seeing her creations so lifeless and limp before her, she found she could not remove them from the earth completely, so using their bones, she transformed them into leopards. The Man-Eaters were allowed to live out the rest of their days in this form, provided that they did not hurt humans unless they were provoked or wounded by one.

Life, Habits, and Friends

The Hadza, much like the San and much like all the ancient African tribes present at the Great Lake, spent countless hours practicing and perfecting their abilities to live in harmony with nature. Even if that relationship was not a concern in their everyday lives, these people did just that. From the moment they were born, from the early hours of the morning to the darkness of the night, these people practiced their languages, hunting abilities, and knowledge of birds and trees and star patterns.

Above all this, the Hadza are most renowned for their

methods of collecting honey. For thousands of years, the Hadza had developed a relationship with the local Honey-Guides, a species of bird found in North Africa that feeds on bugs and bees. They would whistle a tune and the bird would fly down to greet them and lead them toward the nearest hive. The foragers would then light a small fire under the hive to smoke out the bees, and the bird would catch and feed on any stragglers that lingered behind.

Once the hive was clear, the foragers would hack the hive open and collect the honeycomb in their baskets to take home (Giama, 2016).

Living alongside creatures with a heartbeat was not the only means that the Hadza had to survive. They had, through many years, accumulated knowledge of plants, herbs, and their uses.

One particularly useful plant was the desert rose. The Hadza would harvest the stems of the plant and cut them into tiny pieces. They would then boil the cut pieces in a clay pot filled with water and placed them over a fire. The sap would begin to leak out of the stems. They would then remove the plant material and boil the sap further until the liquid dried up, leaving a heavy poison deadly enough to kill a large animal.

The Hadza were capable of more than just herbal remedies and successful hunts, they were excellent shooters. From the age of three, young boys were given their first bow and arrow. From then on, they were expected to practice and play with their tools every day of their lives. As children, they were exceptional, without ever demanding that they be treated as such. They would grow into hunters with vicious accuracy, able to shoot a bird or baboon as it flung through the sky, exactly in the center of the head, every time. Their aim was their deadliest weapon (Lederle, 2014).

The Hadza not only had a good relationship with their environment, but their approach to conflict also put them in good stead with a number of neighboring tribes. Most notable is their relationship with the Isanzu, a Bantu tribe whom they encountered after the Great Bantu Migration.

The Hadza, like many clans, began to suffer the repercussions of climate change at the Great Lake and moved North along with many other local tribes.

After the move, once they had settled further north, the varying groups didn't seem to get in each other's way much at all. In fact, the Hadza came to depend on the local tribes to help mitigate the challenges of their lifestyle. They had a rather close relationship with a Bantu group known as the Isanzu. The Isanzu were pastoralists and had gained herding and farming knowledge from the communities living to the north of Africa when they had first migrated through Africa, years before they had even met the Hadza. Though the Hadza disliked the tediousness of farming, they appreciated the idea of keeping dogs.

The Hadza's relationship with the Isanzu was more than a source of ideas. There are a number of occasions when the Isanzu helped the Hadza through famines by giving them foods and herbs. One such tale of heroism tells the story of how an Isanzu man came into the Hadza lands and died under the conditions that he was met with. But even in death, his love for his neighbors was strong, so he rose from the grave and traveled back to his home, where he collected gifts of meat and honey which he gave to the Hadza, saving them from the plight he had suffered (Madenge, 2021).

Notably, the Hadza had few enemies, unlike their brother tribe, the San.

The Hadza legacy reigned strong with their way of life today, still reflective of their way of life back then.

CHAPTER 4
THE KHOI

The Khoi originated within the surroundings of the Great Lake, a creation that emerged from the mixing of the various clans that resided there. Following the great migration, the Khoi encountered the Bantu most frequently on their way North. Inspired by their pastoral way of life, the Khoi adopted these practices with the indigenous African goats and later, Eurasian cattle. Despite their knowledge of farming, the Khoi were greater herders than they were agriculturists and would often have to move around governing how ripe the land was. When the land became dry or used, the Khoi would move, returning only once the land had become abundant again.

For this reason, their housing structures were small and as easy to put up as they were to take down.

Their herds became a symbol of wealth, where they had once been food without a source of ownership. The Khoi wouldn't use their stock for meat but rather used them as a form of currency. Only on special occasions would the animals be consumed.

For the most part, the Khoi were exceptional hunters and would acquire their daily meat from their surrounding environment—but, the accuracy of their shots dwindled after the adaptations presented by the Bantu. The San and the Hadza would soon become their superiors on the hunting ground. But with the Hadza being overtly friendly and hard to trample over, the San were an easy group to target when issues arose.

Groups and Political Systems

Because the Khoi had cattle and therefore, wealth, they had a caste system separating those who had funds and those who didn't. Like in today's society, the poor struggled through life, claiming work permitted by the rich in an attempt to feed and care for their families and increase their stance in society. The rich, on the other hand, found tradition in marrying and settling beside like-minded individuals and families in order to maintain rank within the caste system.

These beginnings also incorporated the usage and implementation of a chief who controlled and laid out the beliefs, rules, and systems his people would follow.

With any induction of singular leadership, there are bound to be disputes or disagreements so it wasn't uncommon for new systems to escape the clutches of an old society only to start a new one, based on the same principles but governed by different laws.

Such deviations left multiple chiefdoms within one area. The chiefs of each village would often host meetings where they would discuss the availability of resources and how to disperse them as well as any conflict that may have arisen between the different villages.

Despite their willingness to negotiate, the Khoi chiefs were only responsible for their own groups and couldn't always control the actions of the other chiefs and their villages. Thus, the negotiation was a matter of possibility, not regularity.

As with many of the Ancient African groups, the men were hunters and the women were gatherers, except with the Khoi, this was a binding rule. Only the men could hunt, herd and participate in official council business and chiefly negotiations while the women were expected to tend to the homes, take care of the men and their children and forage for food.

Spiritual Beliefs

The Khoi believe in a good god who created Earth and all its creatures. His name was Goab. They also believed in a conflicting deity who controlled evil, sickness, war, and death. His name was Gaunab.

Goab was, at first, a simple plant. When that plant died, he returned as a rabbit. When the rabbit died, he returned as a watering hole, then a hill, then a beetle.

He first became everything that once lived, and then, he became a man.

As a man, Goab was a noble chief. He fought Gaunab on many occasions. Sometimes, he was successful; other times, he and his people would perish. But Goab would return, rising from the dead, to seek the destroyer once more. In his last battle, he used thunder and lightning to defeat Gaunab, bringing long and heavy rains to his people. But the Destroyer was strong and quick and hurtled a large rock at Goab's knee, breaking it.

Goab lives in the sky, tortured by the pain in his leg. Though he cannot be on Earth, he still brings light with the moon in the darkness and rain for his people.

Gaunab still lives on, bringing death and illness to all mankind.

Folktales

The Khoi, like many Ancient African groups, loved to tell folk tales. Some of their stories are about the origins of the land and its creatures, while other tales are about their gods.

The Crane and Its Neck

Once there was a mother Dove who lived on top of a high rock with her small children. One day, a hungry and sly Jackal came past.

Seeing the Dove with her children so high up he said to her, "Give me one of your children, Dove."

The Dove refused, so the Jackal argued, "If you do not give me one, I will fly up there and kill you all."

Terrified, the Dove agreed and threw one of her babies down for the Jackal to take.

The next day, the Jackal returned, and again, the Dove gave up one of her children.

The Dove cried after the Jackal had left, catching the attention of the Crane.

"Why do you cry?" the Crane asked.

"The Jackal comes here every day for one of my children. If I refuse him, he shall fly up here and kill them all," she explained.

The Crane shook his head.

"You have been fooled, Jackals cannot fly."

With that, the Crane left.

The Jackal came back the next day and asked for one of the Dove's babies.

"The Crane said that you cannot fly. I will not give you any more," said the Dove.

Angered, the Jackal went to see the Crane and, creeping up behind him, cracked his neck.

To this day, the Crane has a crooked neck.

The Hare and Its Lip

After his death, Goab found sanctuary in the sky, where he could spend his days in silence, mourning his wounded knee. He sent word to the Moon to have a letter written and sent to the people. The Moon called upon the Hare, one of his greatest admirers, and tasked the Hare with writing the following:

"As I am dying and rising again, so too are you dying and rising again."

It was a simple letter, but the Hare, in its hurry, got confused and wrote:

"As I am dying and rising again, so too are you dying and not rising again."

The Hare delivered the message to the people and returned to the moon to tell of the expedition. The moon was very angry at the Hare's foolishness and slapped him in the face with a stick, splitting the hare's lip.

To this day, the hare has a split lip.

Life, Habits, and Friends

Since the Khoi and the Bantu shared similarities, the groups often got on rather well. This led to a mass expansion of mineral wealth owned by the Khoi such as copper and iron, all resources brought by the Bantu from their migration through Europe. Along with these, gold, beads, cloth, and oils were other commonly traded goods between the groups.

But if the groups had such great ties, what could lead the Bantu to chase the Khoi out of North Africa, all the way to the southern coast?

Multiple factors governed the systems that had to fall in order for that to happen.

Firstly, the effect of climate change on the Khoi caused internal conflicts to stir. As their environment changed, the locals predicted that the rules would change with it, but they didn't, and many of the youth left to create clans of their own. This expanded the area that the Khoi were traversing remarkably and led to the settlement of Khoi in various Bantu states, some of which were accepting, and many of which were not.

The Khoi had always been a people who wanted to share their beliefs with the world and bring outsiders under their wings. The Bantu, equally proud people, confronted outsiders with the same outlook. This, mixed with the diminishing size of the various clans and the increasing level of disorganization within them, led to external conflicts, which the Khoi often could not defend themselves.

With resources dwindling because of the drying up of the environment, their expansion on one hand and their need to navigate into occupied territory to feed their livestock led to further confrontations that wouldn't have happened so quickly had the environment been tamer.

Hungry and ungoverned, the Khoi found themselves

prey in a land that they once controlled. Those who hadn't been killed or swept up into other tribes through marriage or slavery, fled, settling in the South. This turbulent time led to the creation of a Bantu-Khoi combination group, the Korana.

The Korana

In the 1830s, the Korana was ruled by Gert Hooyman (Kora, n.d.). He led his people through the lands of a Bantu subgroup, the Ndebele tribe. During this time, the Ndebele were being ruled by the powerful Mzilikazi. While passing through, there was no sign of the fearsome army that had been reported by the neighboring tribes, and so the group fancied themselves content in the home of their enemies.

At the time, Mzilikazi was feared as much as he was respected. He had come from the Great Zulu Kingdom and had been a close companion of Shaka, King of the Zulus, a subbranch of the Bantus that chose to reside in central Africa after the Great Migration. The Bantus, like the Khoi, saw cattle as a form of wealth. Shaka would frequently send his warriors out to raid the lands for these precious creatures. One day, after a successful raid, Mzilikazi chose to go against his friend and keep all the cattle for himself. He left, taking his followers as far away from the Zulu Kingdom as he could, in fear of the retribution he might suffer. Once they had settled in the southern parts of Africa, Mzilikazi, like Shaka, raided the surrounding tribes and expanded his territory. His men grew strong and fought as valiant warriors do. Still, to those around them, they were seen as thieves, tricksters, and murderers. Most swore never to stand in their path.

Perhaps, though, it was all baseless rumor. Having come from the far north, Hooyman could not be sure if the tales told to him by prisoners of lost tribes were true or simply a means of distraction.

As they passed through the land, the Korana raided the cattle available, herding some and slaughtering others for meat. After all, unprotected cattle might as well have no value.

Together Hooyman and his people feasted on the meat, cooking and eating it in the clear and serene location once believed to be owned by true warriors.

While he feasted, two Ndebele women found him. Taken by his kindness and humor the women chose to warn him that he was not alone. Mzilikazi's great army was away raiding another tribe but the Ndebele elders were present and in hiding and would wait until he and his followers fell asleep to slaughter them.

Hooymen and his people scoured the land but it was completely empty.

Perhaps the women had tried to fool him into leaving? Perhaps they were afraid his people would harm them? Or perhaps they were hiding cattle elsewhere and didn't want him to find it.

Nonetheless, he couldn't see a reason not to stay, and with no sign of the great army's return, he and his people settled in for the night.

But, it would prove that the women truly had tried to warn him as in the depth of the Korana slumber, the veterans came and slaughtered them all.

Thousands of bodies lay on the once serene landscape, bloody and cold. Later, their skeletons would chill the bones of passersby, a deadly reminder of Mzilikazi's strength.

To this day, the place of the murder is called Moordkop and though no marking resides there to commemorate the Girque lost, they are remembered by those who managed to escape and later settle in Namibia and the Cape.

The San

The Khoi that remained independent channeled parallel to the Korana, both of them making their way to the cape. The Korana survivors of the Ndebele people met the last of the Khoi there. Together they were introduced to the San.

Though the groups first attempted to get along well, the San had a different way of life from the two groups. They were not herders, they were hunter-gatherers and to them, the land and its creatures were not something one could own. Seeing cattle in kraal meant little to them other than that their families would be fed and they wouldn't have to suffer organizing and following through on a hunt. This mindset shadowed their inevitable theft of the Korana and the Khoi crops and resources.

Angered, the Khoi and the Korana battled and trifled with the San people, pushing survivors further inland while incorporating the slow-legged among their own people. First, the San were used as slaves and traded between the two tribes. Over time, the San members were accepted in the community and given Khoi wives. Thus, the combination of the Korana, Khoi, and San peoples led to the formation of the Khoisan.

CHAPTER 5
PYGMY PEOPLE

Once upon a time, there was a father who had three sons, Katutsi, Kahutu, and Katwa. The father was ill and wanted to give his three sons a piece of his heritage before he passed. He decided he would delegate his belongings based on how responsible each of his children was and so, he came up with a test.

One night, he gave each of his sons full bottles of milk to take care of. When he woke in the morning, he found that Katutsi's bottle was full, Kahutu's bottle was half full, and Katwa's bottle was empty.

In recognition of the care taken to preserve the milk within the bottles, the father gifted Katutsi all his herds to use and enjoy for generations to come. Kahutu was gifted all of his seeds so that he and his future families could grow their own foods lastly, Katwa was given a forest where he and his family would have to hunt and forage for their meals.

That is how the Pygmy people view their beginnings, but the historical findings of how they originated is a far more saddening and delicate matter.

From the beginning of time, people have rejected individuals who were different. The Hadza and the San, like many groups, had individuals who looked and acted differently from the rest. These individuals were reasonably shorter in height and smaller in build. Their odd appearance meant that finding romantic companionship and marriage among those who were taller and stronger was difficult, if not impossible. These individuals, seen as the outcasts of their society, left if they weren't banished to live out their days in solitude.

Amazingly, it wasn't just one or two who got left out from their initial groups; rather, there were hundreds and thousands of these outcasts. This group of outcasts banded together, finding solitude in the quiet serenity of the forests, and became known as the Batwa people.

Groups and Political Systems

1000 B.C.E. entertained a variety of different forest life, and where there was forest, there was the Batwa (Kwekudee, 2013). The distance between these forestry locations, although vast, never led to much friction between the local groups. Throughout Africa, the differently located Batwa groups followed the same beliefs, religions, habits, and policies.

Batwa people, like the San and the Hadza, were hunter-gatherers. However, their smaller inhabitation, as forests, for the most part, were in comparison to dry land, didn't make them more accurate or valiant hunters than the taller surrounding tribespeople. They were hunter-gatherers of average skill and gentle-minded people who struggled immensely when taken out of their green homes.

A group of Batwa within a forest was subdivided into clans or families. The clans would settle close to one another, and participate in evening entertainment together, hunting, and marital debates, but, for the most part, the families lived and survived independently of one another.

The Batwa were mostly monogamous and, in comparison to their surrounding tribes, relied heavily on the authority of women when it came to managing households and everyday difficulties.

This is not to say that women in Batwa society had a higher standing than men. Men were still placed in positions of major authority, but the Batwa held the female identified in higher regard than that of other tribes.

For the Batwa, the women made many of the household decisions and often had a say in grouped clan meetings. This is because women mostly stayed behind at the settlement to fish and gather food while the men went off hunting. Thus, the time they spent at the settlement was more than the men and allowed for the women to have had a better understanding of the disputes that needed settling within these areas.

In addition, because the women were in close proximity to the homes during the day, they were expected to cook, clean, take care of and educate the children as well as managing household finances and clan resources. This made them pivotal in the Pygmy society and valued members when it came to decision-making.

The opinions of the women could be voiced during the council of elders, which was held every so often when domestic disputes became large enough to require mediation. The council of elders was built up of the oldest people within each family clan. A Chief, usually the oldest out of the gentlemen, would lead the discussions, enforcing that every person had equal say.

What was inherently sad, was that these pivotal members of Batwa society were often taken for granted by neighboring, unrelated tribesmen. The Batwa woman was frequently kidnapped and abused, leaving them and their families paralyzed and without a medium for decision-making.

Over time, these groups of beautiful people suffered great illnesses and strife at the hands of brutal neighbors, who even today, take advantage of the surviving peoples, hurt them and prolong their suffering.

Spiritual Beliefs

The Batwa had no religious belief systems. Rather, they worshiped the forest in which they lived, claiming the space as their parents and themselves as the children of the forest.

The Batwa learned many things from their green parents, such as ancient medicinal knowledge. It was the herbology and healing techniques that had even their greatest of enemies falling onto their knees for access to their great, life-saving skills. The Batwa were exceptional healers and helped the Egyptians using the plants found within their homelands.

For their medicines, creams, edibles, and inhalants, they commonly used roots, tree bark, a variety of plant matter, and items such as gorilla bones.

Their years of practice in herbology had given the Batwa people one item of trade that every surrounding tribe wanted. Where their enemies begged them for assistance, their friends, mostly found amongst Egyptians, were gifted this knowledge without hesitation.

Though it seemed only the Egyptians could see it, the Batwa truly were remarkable people, and when it came to saving the lives of others, they truly did seem to perform the impossible. With these abilities, it is no wonder that their enemies feared and despised them. How could anyone compete with a group that seemed to have the knowledge to bring back the dead?

Folktales

Cannibals

Tales of the Batwa people have been told for centuries, depicting the people as fantastical, cannibalistic people.

Why spread such rumors, especially when the Pygmies are some of the most peaceful and poorly treated people in Africa?

The rumors began thousands of years ago, after the Great Migration. The Pygmies' forests were filled with rerouting peoples, Khoi tribes, and Bantu groups. Each of these groups brought with them goods that could be used for trade.

The Batwa were not, at this point, scattered all over the continent. They resided in one area. Their skill for medicinal practices was yearned for by many who wanted to get the best deal that they could out of Batwa healers. The prices for the medicine were low and maintained by keeping trespassers out of that route.

Tradesmen would whisper words of horror and sacrilege to anyone who dared mention the Batwa name in the hopes that they would be too scared to go and look for the group. If there was no competition, the traders could continue to get more for what they were willing to give.

The Batwa were said to be cannibals who had a special place where they would fatten and rub down enemies and trespassers with herbs and oils. They would then cook their meat above a fire and invite the family of their meal to dine with them in a specific hut where they would be shoved, and held down in their seats while their loved ones were served whole on a silver dish. There was no way these victims could escape, for the pygmies had men everywhere, watching their every move. Their teeth were sharp, and their bodies were covered in holes dug by forks, making them look ten times more terrifying. There would be no confrontation or escape. There would only be tears and pain as the family was forced to dine with their captives, eating the bodies of those passed. After the meal, they would be taken to the special place where their loved ones had been. They would be chained and anointed, prepared for the next meal.

This farfetched tale is far from the truth, though there are elements of the story that ring true. But to understand what really happened, we need to trace a timeline of the Great Migration and all those whom the Batwa encountered. For it is in these tales of encounter that the bitter truth to this rumor can be uncovered.

Life, Habits, and Friends

As the Great Migration began, and the various groups began to flee from the ripening climate change toward new hopes and new locations, the Pygmies stayed. Their forest had hardly been tampered with. The sun was not bright enough to destroy the insides, and they never relied on the dwindling resources of the climate outside. They had found peace in their home and solitude away from the rejection and snubs from the other groups. Here, they had everything they needed.

Unfortunately, they also had everything the outsiders wanted.

The Bantu, the first known trespassers, entered the forests and saw the potential for farming, hunting, and a better, cooler life. Though they were further away from freshwater, the majority of their wealth being cattle, allowed them to easily transport refreshments to and from the drying lake. They had a wild game, grass for their livestock, and fertile land. There was just one problem.

The Batwa were hunter-gatherers. They didn't believe in land ownership. The Batwa would often strike at the Bantu's cattle and the Bantu would seek retribution, often to devastating effects.

The Bantu, by this point, had a well-organized political system that was controlled by one person who could make and abandon rules to satisfy their beliefs and the needs of their people. There were no counter spokesmen to help rework violent thinking.

On most occasions, the chiefs would send out their warriors to kill the Batwa people.

The men would bring back trophies of their conquests, as was the trend in any successful raid, and the group would marvel at the strange appearance of the Pygmy people.

The Bantu groups started to see the Batwa people as

subhuman.

Still, the Batwa fought back, with all the strength they could muster. This was not just their home. They were spiritually attached to their forests, claiming the land as kin. They were devastated and enraged by the Bantus' destruction of it to make way for farming settlements.

They would strike arrows in the Bantus' hearts, and the Bantus would club and hack at their flesh in return.

In the end, the small stature of the Batwa was no match for the Bantu. Those who happened to be just out of reach, cowardly while they watched their neighbors die. Others fled. The group split into four with participants traveling east, north, and south. Those who remained moved only a few miles west to make room for their new neighbors.

The bodies of the dead were mutilated and eaten. The Bantus' victories over the strange-looking people made them think that the Batwa held some kind of magic. They believed that by eating the flesh of the Batwa, they might grow strong and be cured of their ailments.

Those that had been captured were enslaved, and the families that remained offered up their youth for the same purpose in trade for peace.

And so began one of the very first accounts of slavery. The Bantu group that had invaded the area had come to own the Batwa people and their children. Should those children marry and give birth, those children would be owned by the Bantu.

As time went on and the now separate groups began to settle in their new locations, each of them began to adapt to the traditions of their neighbors. This group was called the Ngombe. The Ngombe began to hunt and cannibalize their own people, and in doing so, were banished from the clan lineage.

To this day, the Ngombe is widely represented as the Bantu people.

Their allegiance to the Bantu and betrayal of their own allowed them to escape the ruins of their once peaceful home. They moved south, settling alongside their old Batwa lineages as they tried to rekindle their once close relationship.

In many ways, the Ngombe was able to find forgiveness and friendship among their neighbors, though never again would they be considered brothers. Even today, they are held accountable for what they did. As if reminders from neighboring clans weren't enough, the Ngombe themselves shiver at their past and try not to speak of their gruesome history.

One might hope that over thousands of years, the relationship between the Bantu and Batwa has improved. However, that is not the case. Rather, many pygmies are still enslaved to Bantu masters and ridiculed publicly by the Bantu people. Similarly, the Bantu are attacked and murdered by the Batwa.

For the rich on either side, a celebration is not joyous

without the bloodshed of their enemies. Weddings, births, and funerals all dictate to an extent the killing of local enemies.

Their Venture

Once they had migrated out of their homes, the Batwa changed and adapted to the traditions of their neighboring tribes and their landscape, cultivating four distinct subgroups, each with their own way of speaking and their own philosophies around religion and origin.

Batwa in the South

The Batwa were the first to settle along the land now known as Rwanda. They made their home in the comfort of the forests that resided there, for that was how they were used to living. They gathered berries and honey and hunted the game that lived among them, and for some time, it felt as though their past would simply be just that, the past.

Except that the past has a nasty habit of repeating itself.

After a few hundred years, the Hutu and the Tutsi arrived on land that is now part of Rwanda. The Hutu were herders, while the Tutsi were agriculturalists. Neither of the groups found comfort in living in the forest, so they began to destroy any means of it that would prevent them from living in the ways that they were used to.

Soon, the Tutsis had developed a monarchy, stronger

than any of the groups in the area. They began to rule over the land and its inhabitants, including the Hutu and the Pygmies, whose value in the society began to dwindle. The Pygmies, as always, were placed at the bottom of the caste system. However, they had learned from their ancestors' mistakes and weren't willing to make the same mistake again. Though some were taken as slaves, many offered their services to the Tutsi king. They would work as spies, warriors, entertainers, and medicinal healers as well as tradesmen for the monarchy.

With the new influences that surrounded them, the Batwa's belief systems and religious practices changed. They came to believe that a supreme being called Imaana created all the earth and its creatures. He was a loving and humorous god who loved children and enjoyed games. In the beginning, Imaana blessed his people with immortality. However, he found his enemy, Death, was working against his people too often. Hating watching his creations rise from their graves over and over, Imaana sought to destroy Death. He warned the people to stay away and hide. But one old lady, unloved by her family with only her garden to warm her heart, left her hiding place to fetch vegetables. Death found her and hid under her skirt. Once the old lady had gone home, he killed her and swept through her village, causing chaos among the people.

All might have awoken the following day if it wasn't for the old lady's daughter, who despised her. The girl threw barrels of sand over the old woman's grave so that she might not leave her resting place.

The next day, the girl came back and poured more sand on the old lady's grave.

She hadn't noticed the effect she was having on the potency of immortality for those around her.

On the third day, she came back and discovered that there were no signs of movement. The old lady had been rested for eternity, and so, too, had the gift of immortality.

To this day, the people shy away from death, hiding in the forests and in small huts. When a family member dies, the relatives move and take special herbs to blind the ghost of the departed from sensing them and joining the family in their new home.

Imaana flew away into the sky, for he blamed himself for the loss the people had suffered. The only one he lets close to him is the chameleon, who sits high in the tree and radiates within Imaana's splendor.

Mbuti in the Eastern Congo

The Mbuti, like the other Batwa tribes, settled in the forests of Sudan and were granted just enough time to forget their strife before they were surrounded by Bantu villages. The Mbuti found themselves living a dual existence, one in which they followed the rules of their rulers and the village folk and partook in their traditions, and a second in which they remained the unchained, free folk of the forest.

The Mbuti very cleverly adapted to the Bantu way of life when they were in the open. They lived in more permanent huts where they selected a chief who would be responsible for negotiating disputes with the surrounding villages. The chief was usually an elder who got on well with those respective communities. However, once they entered the forests for rituals, celebrations, hunting, or general enjoyment, there was no chief, and the people reverted to an egalitarian society.

The same rules were applied with regard to arranged marriages forced by Bantu rulers. The couple would accept the instruction and enjoy a lavish feast sponsored by the ruler on their wedding day. However, once they returned to the forest, they were not wed, would not share a bed, and could love whom they desired.

The Mbuti never lost the spiritual awareness their ancestors shared with the forest and continued to claim the space as being both their maternal and paternal kin. To them, the forest would forever be a sacred place.

CHAPTER 6
ISRAELITES IN AFRICA

The Israelites started making their way into Africa by following the Nile river from Asia and through Egypt, all the way to North Africa, where they settled in Nubia. Here, the Israelites began to mix with the strains of Bantu that were beginning to flow through the same channel at about the same time. These combinations would create the first Egyptians

Ancient Egypt

The very first ruler of ancient Egypt was originally thought to be a pharaoh called Ro. However, recent excavations have shown that this translation may be wrong. Rather, the hieroglyphics translate the name as 'Big Mouth' or chief.

The first chief of ancient Egypt was succeeded by Ka, the first known pharaoh of the mystical land of Thinis, which was the capital of Lower Egypt.

Narmer succeeded Ka and had the goal of uniting Upper and Lower Egypt.

Narmer had a son called Menes, who succeeded him when he died. During Menes' reign, he started cultivating the origins of ancient Egyptian hieroglyphics and beliefs by creating the well-known ankh and the djed pillar symbols. These symbols revealed the ancient Egyptians' understanding of mortality and the afterlife. They believed that the spirit could enjoy two existences, one in the world of the living and one in the world of the dead.

Menes later conquered and claimed Memphis as the Egyptian capital. It would be the seat of the Egyptian government for the next several dynasties.

Hor Ahai was the next Pharaoh. He was named after Horus, the Egyptian god of the sky. Egyptian folklore has it that Horus was the son of Isis, who birthed him after she had received the butchered body parts of her philandering husband, Osiris. Seth, his brother, and his murderer—as well as the God of disorder—had drowned him after he learned that Osiris had had an affair with Seth's wife and their fellow sister, and left her pregnant with a child, who she called Anubis. Seth then chopped up Osiris' body and threw his penis into the water.

Egypt expanded dramatically during the 26 dynasties that would come. By that time, Pharaoh Psamtik the second would change the capital of ancient Egypt from Memphis to the Meroe Empire. The Meroe Empire was quickly reclaimed as the land of Kush.

Batwa in Egypt

The Egyptians first noticed these short, miraculous people to the south of the Nile and instantly took to them. They found something magical and wonderful about the way the Batwa people spoke, walked, and looked. To the Egyptians, the Batwa were a source of good luck and hope, and the Egyptians would regularly try to invite Batwa to Egyptian meetings and affairs. The Batwa and the Egyptians had a trusting friendship, with the Batwa being paid generous wages to work as advisors to the pharaohs. Finally, these amazing people had found a group who accepted them for who they were.

Kingdom of Kush

Kush was mostly ruled by powerful queens who were not only responsible for the people of Nubia but were responsible for the lives and ranks of their sons as they tried to push them atop the Egyptian throne. It is said that the land of Kush is where the Queen of Sheba ruled for a time before she met and dabbled in romance with Solomon, who produced her as an heir.

The Kingdom of Kush was later called the Aksumite Empire.

The very first queen of the Aksumite Empire was Shanakdakheto, who was appointed by her supposed son, Psamtic II. Shortly after their rise, they met and welcomed the Romans into their lands. The Romans, through trading with the Greeks, harped upon North Africa. Seeing the abundance of agriculture and life that sprouted from the ripe soils of the Nile, the Romans were eager to start trading with the locals.

The effects of the Romans on the Egyptians and the local Bantu tribes would be huge and last right up until modern times. During their encounters, the Romans tried to conquer Egypt many times.

Carthage

Carthage was a city and trading port built by the Canaanites as they fled from Yahweh and his followers after being declared sinners against the one true God. Carthage flourished with its close proximity to Israelite, Greek, and Roman traders. However, Rome was becoming increasingly powerful. Having seen Carthage's good relationships with so many other nations, the Egyptian land resources, and the 200 trading docks existing within, they decided to conquer it.

This led to the rise of the three Punic Wars in which Julius Caesar tried desperately to colonize the capital. On his third attempt, he succeeded and laid claim to the once-proud trading station.

Queen Amanirenas was the ruler of the Aksumite Empire when the Romans finally achieved their goal and were looking to expand even further inland. With bravery and courage, she defended her people and set out on an attack in which she conquered the Romans that had taken control of Southern Egypt.

The Romans would retaliate for the next two years, progressively pushing Amanirenas and her people further inland. Amanrienas was not one to give up, but after years of fighting and having lost her husband and son to the Roman Empire, she grew tired and was eventually defeated.

The Romans could have ruled over Egypt but chose not to. The Egyptian way of life, the heat, and the terrain did not appeal to their habits or understanding. They were incapable of living there and growing weaker by the day, so they left.

CHAPTER 7
THE BANTU

The Bantu were a colorful semantic-speaking group of various ethnicities that entered Africa through Asian channels. Having come from a long lineage of Homo-Sapiens that traveled outside of Africa for a time, they brought with them a wealth of knowledge that the indigenous tribes didn't have. These behaviors and ways of life influenced the locals in a variety of ways. For one, the Bantu's political organizational systems were far more intense, guided, and yielded faster results than the systems within the local groups. This, along with their knowledge in farming and herding as well as combat, made the Bantu an exceptionally powerful force. They too followed the Nile river, progressively moving further inland toward where they would find, the Great Lake.

The Great Bantu Migration and the Kingdom of Zimbabwe

The four major subgroups of the Bantu speakers are the Venda, Nguni, and the Shangaan-Tsonga. After the temperatures began to rise at the Great Lake. The Shangaan-Tsonga moved south along the east coast of Central Africa, the Venda moved along with them but chose to take a more inland channel and the Nguni stayed in the center but moved south and were subsequently the first group to reach the Southern African border. These groups then spread out as they tried to find suitable land to farm and keep their cattle. This meant that the groups often bumped into one another. Such encounters had a way of molding the emergence of new groups and new hatred. Some myths suggest that the encounter between the Venda and the Nguni people created the Sotho-Tswana.

Mapungubwe

The first child born from the mixture between the Shongaan and the Nguni was Thobela. Once he had reached a ripe age, he chose to abandon his family lineage and begin his own dynasty. As the Shongaan and the Nguni moved on, he stayed behind with his followers, the Karanga, and began to build a kingdom known as Mapungubwe in Lesotho.

One day, the settlers found a shiny speck of dust on the surface of the earth. It glittered in the sun and made for fine jewelry and decorations. They found that heating this mineral over a fire would melt it down and make it more adaptable. They integrated this metal into their everyday lives. Only later would they learn that they had found gold.

It wasn't long before the Karanga was attacked and conquered by the Venda under King Shiriyadenga. The survivors that managed to escape moved west toward Botswana, where they built a similar kingdom called Khami.

Shiriyadenga ruled the dual tribes of the Venda and the Karanga with majestic grace, so much so that the people began to believe that his home was a sacred place, controlled and adorned by the ancestors. To speak ill about it would be disrespectful, as it would agitate the spirits.

Venda Culture and Spiritual Beliefs

For the Venda, spirits were everywhere. Spirits of the dead lingered long after one's passing, and the spirits of the cave and the water could bring about your doom as well as your greatest joys.

The Venda believed in many gods. The most powerful was the Rhaluvimba, a golden bird of light that brought lightning and thunder. Their second most powerful god was the Sacred Python, a mythical snake that lived beneath the water and controlled the water sprites and ancestral spirits that lived within. When the water rose high, the locals would quickly get to higher ground and leave the sick and old behind. This was because they believed that the Python was sending his sprites to take those souls to a new life under the water. It was merciful and kind to leave them to the fate of their God.

The locals took care to worship their gods correctly, and their gods responded with adoration, gifting the people with an abundance of crops such as coffee, tea, beans, peas, and wheat that they could farm. For meat, the people would kill their local birds, cattle, goats, and sheep.

Roles within the walls of Mapumgubwe were specific and unwavering. Women were to tend to the fields and take care of the children, while the men would take care of the poultry, hunting, herding, and politics.

The Year of Hunger

An old Venda folk tale goes like this:

The animals had been starving, and the baboons were the most hungry of all.

"What can we do?" they asked each other as they watched the humans eat and dance with great joy.

"We need to send someone very pretty to marry the king of those people; maybe then she can send us back some food."

At that moment, the beautiful young Unyamaleli walked past. Her family grabbed her and skinned her alive.

Cold and scared, she agreed to follow along with their plan. She would go to the village, seduce the king, and marry him. Then she would steal mielie from the homestead and leave some in a pot by the river for her family to eat.

She went to the village, and the king was taken by her beauty. They were married, and she began to steal the mielie for her family and leave it for them to eat.

She did this for some time until she feared that the other wives were getting suspicious, so she stopped.

"Look at her over there, so rich, plump, and happy. It is as if she has forgotten us." Her family said.

"We must teach her a lesson."

All the baboons in the family could play musical instruments, so they picked up their crafts and began to sing.

The king was so taken by the singing that he invited everyone to come and listen and watch the baboons perform.

Unyamaleli didn't want to join in as she recognized it was the voices of her estranged family.

The King told her to come and enjoy the performance because it was making everyone happy, so she was forced to watch.

Her family loomed closer and closer until they snatched back Unyamaleli's skin and threw her back into her old one.

"Oh my god," said the king. "I've been married to a

baboon."

This folktale is a reminder of how the Venda families address issues in their households (A Venda Folktale, n.d.).

Khami

The Karanga rebuilt their empire in the Kingdom of Khami. Khami, in many ways, was similar to Mapungubwe, with fertile ground, a good water supply, mountains of gold, and abundant plant life for their cattle to enjoy.

Khami was built of stone, as was Mapungubwe, but pictures of Khami depict much stronger, thicker walls as if the Karanga at the time were nervous about another invasion.

They had every right to be, as not far from them lived a budding Shongaan clan known as the Rozvi. It wasn't long before the Rozvi attacked the Karanga people at Khami and claimed the kingdom for the Rozvi dynasty.

Karanga (Tswana) Culture and Spiritual Beliefs

The ancient Karanga were peaceful people. They believed that everything that they saw before them was cultivated by their ancestors. The earth was the back of their departed loved ones and was, therefore, very sacred and fragile. Taking the land and its creatures for granted was considered deeply taboo, as was the idea of war and bloodshed. They didn't believe that the earth was something that could be sold, owned, or kept.

"Have this land," a Karanga might say. But what they mean is, "I don't mind you staying here. It doesn't bother me, so long as the ancestors are happy, and my people are unharmed. I will reside here too. If I need, I may use this land as you may use mine. You may give this land to another, and I will still be here if it suits me and you and whomever you have given it to."

This understanding of the land would become a dangerous source of misunderstanding between the Karanga and ambitious African kings.

The Karanga aimed to live in harmony with their world so much that certain behaviors and habits were considered taboo. One was not allowed to kill crocodiles, elephants, or leopards, or they would strike misfortune on themselves and their clans. People weren't allowed to fetch water with dirty clay pots; they had to wash them first, or the stream and the rivers would die. Moreover, certain plants and trees like the baobab were not to be cut down or harvested for their fruits or produce.

Monomotapa Empire

The Rozvi were the ruling clan within a great Shogaan empire called Monomotapa. The King, Changamira, was known to be brave, resourceful, and a good warrior. He planned to expand his reign as far as he could and in doing so, conquered Mapungubwe from Shiriyadenga and Khami from the Karanga and pulled them under his empire.

Shona Culture and Spiritual Beliefs

The Venda and the Tswana are both subgroups of the Shona people. The Shona believed in a supreme being who they called Mwari. Mwari was neither a male nor a female, rather it was a power that lived in the sky. Mwari created the earth and all its creatures for reasons of his own. He didn't like to discuss those reasons with anyone. It was considered rude to question why Mwari did the things he did. Though, for the most part, he had everyone's best interest at heart, sending rain when the people needed it and hope when it seemed lost.

Mwari was not always reachable, so the people would communicate with the ancestors of their departed loved ones and the spirits of the earth.

These spirits could bring good luck or bad, depending on which person was communicating with them and whether or not they were displeased or happy. Illness and death were believed to be the cause of witchcraft and angered spirits.

The Tribal healers had the best connection with these entities and hours of agonized herbal medicinal practice. The healers would throw bones to conjure the thoughts and ideas of the ancestors in order to make a prognosis and set about a remedy.

Then, they would make offerings to the spirits in the forms of food, beer, and meat to try and appease them and gather their interest in healing the sick.

The Shona, like many African groups, were organized through a system of certified male and female roles.

The Shona were polygamists, so the husband would live with the mother and child of his first wife and follow a visiting schedule between his other wives and families. The first wife was responsible for handling internal disputes, while the husband was responsible for training the young boys for fighting.

Kings were positioned through a line of descent, with the firstborn son of the first wife being the heir to the throne. Once the king had passed, the rightful heir would be claimed King and rule among his father's following, while his brothers would rule alongside him as separate chieftains. The king was a title given to the firstborn. But, the position came with the same responsibilities as any chieftaincy.

When a new king was born a group of young boys was sent to work for the new princely household. By the time the king came of age, the boys who once helped change the royal babe's diapers had become his respected counselors, older, wiser, and more knowledgeable about the king than even he might be. These counselors would group together regularly to try to find means of handling the disputes between the chieftains, often to no avail.

Folktales

Senseless Murder

A well-known folktale told by the Shona is the story about the Lion and the Hare...

One day, Lion asks the Hare if he will care for and feed his three children while he goes out hunting in strange forests. The hare agrees, so Lion goes.

While out hunting, Lion catches a bird and yells out for the Hare. The Hare's face pops up from far away.

"Here is some meat," yelled Lion, and he threw the meal to the Hare, who jumped up to grab it.

"Are my children alright?" Lion then asked.

"Yes," replied the hare, so the Lion continued on his way.

But the Hare was hungry, so he ate the bird.

The next day, Lion didn't catch anything, but at the end of the day, he still called out to the hare.

The hare's head popped up from far, far away.

"Are my children alright?" he asked.

"Yes," replied the hare, so Lion went on his way.

But the hare was very hungry, so he ate one of the cubs.

The third day, the Lion caught a snake and called out to Hare.

The Hare popped up from far, far, far away.

"Here is some meat for you," the Lion said and threw the meal to the Hare.

"Are my children alright?" he then asked.

"Yes," said the Hare, so Lion carried on with his hunt.

The Hare sighed at the small piece of meat he had been thrown.

That cub was so much meatier, he thought, so he ate the snake and one more cub.

The next day, the Lion didn't catch anything but still called out to the Hare.

The Hare popped up from far, far, far, far away.

"Are my children alright?" Lion asked.

"Yes," said the Hare, so Lion carried on with the hunt.

But the Hare had grown used to his meal and decided to eat the last cub.

When the Lion returned and found his children gone, he asked the Hare what had happened.

The Hare blamed the deaths of the Lion's children on the baboons, and thus started a series of senseless killings (Makaudze, 2013).

The Nguni, Shona, Venda and Tswana (Karanga) movements

Shortly after their encounter with the Venda and their growing Monomotapa empire, the Nguni made a race toward the Vaal River. But, it was too late, the Venda cultural and linguistic impact on their group had caused many conflicts within the group, and the Nguni's split in half with one staying behind and the other moving eastward toward Mozambique.

The Nguni found peace here for a little while before the conflict in the group drove them to split again. As one stayed behind in the Mozambique area, the other moved east, toward the coast, where they would encounter the Shona people.

Something sparked in these two groups, they got on well, so made companions of each other as they continued to move southward through the Lebombo mountains where they would settle in a beautiful and mystical land, called Embo.

What Embo was like and what occurred there to make the groups shift again is still a mystery.

The people of Embo moved southwards toward Swaziland, where they broke apart into three separate entities.

The Ngwane occupied Swaziland under Chief Sobhuza the first.

The Ndwandwe, the second group, moved back toward Embo and settled on the west along the Pongola borders, where they started to build the Kingdom of Zwide.

The third of the three Embo groups moved South. Conflict eventually split the group down the middle. The first of the two groups settled to the south of the Drakensberg Mountains and formed the Bele-Zizi people, while the other moved south, settling in the

Transkei as the Mpondo people.

The second half of the Nguni group that had split away and halted in Mozambique, moved south toward Natal. It is here that the Mtethwa settled between the Mseleni and the Mhlatuzi Rivers, where they created the Dingiswayo Empire.

After a disagreement with his father, the Chief of the Mtetwa people, Chief Malendela rebelled and moved into Zululand where he began the Zulu Empire which would be ruled under Chief Chama, followed by his son, Senzangakhona and later, the greatest African leader of all time, Shaka Zulu.

The Nguni who had escaped the clutches of the Venda and had settled along the Vaal River moved south-east toward the Drakensberg where the Bele-Zizi had settled and established themselves as the Xhosa and the Thembu. The two groups passed through unscathed and settled alongside the Mpondo with the Xhosa placing themselves in the highlands.

Kingdom of Sofala

Shortly after the migrations from the Great Lake, the Arabs arrived and began trading their gold, copper, and spices with the now mixed Khoisan tribe. For the most part, the group was on good terms with the Khoisan, who helped them move farther inland and where they built a trading port.

A few years later, the group was joined by a subclan of the Karanga that was known as the Ghoya who also established good relations with the Arabs.

With the Khoi helping from time to time but residing happily in the cape, the Ghoya settled next to their new allies.

The Arabs, settling into their new home, found bounties of gold underground. They were as quick to pass on the word to their new friends and explain the minerals' relevance as they were to inform their friends outside of Africa, the Portuguese.

Mining stations and ports were developed with the Khoi and Ghoya working for the Arabs in return for gold and rich minerals.

A short while after settling, the combined Arab, Khoisan, and Ghoya friendship was put to the test when the intruding Karanga and Batonga people, descendants of the Shangaan-Tsonga people, attacked and conquered them.

The Portuguese, arriving on the scene a short while later, was dazed by the ongoing battles of medieval central Africa.

The Portuguese themselves were quickly swept up under King Changamira Ratvi's reign within the Monomotapa Empire.

As Changamira claimed ownership over the surrounding clans, so thus ended what was the Great Kingdom of Zimbabwe.

Changamira went on to establish good relations with

the Venda, the Arabs, and the Portuguese, but the Ghora and the Karanga were enslaved.

With the industries of Portugal and Arabia expanding rapidly, the Ghora became valuable.

From the Portuguese, Changamira acquired fighting knowledge and a large mielie crop. From the Arabs, he procured fine silks, spices, and animals such as the Basenji dog.

Changamira's reign in the Kingdom of Sofala was quickly ended once the Portuguese decided that they wanted more.

CHAPTER 8
SWAZILAND

A History of the Ngwane People

The Ngwane People found unification in their home under the leadership of King Sobhuza In the early 1800s (Gillis, 1999). King Sobhuza's followers were not numerous, and alliances need to be built in order to keep out the Dingiswayo and Sotho raiders. King Sobhuza managed to form contracted alliances with the Dingiswayo empire by marrying the daughters of the Mthethwa chief, Dingiswayo, and the daughter of the Ndwandwe leader, Chief Zwide.

However, his alliance with the Ndwandwe people didn't last long as climate change forced the lakes in Africa to dry up. Without water, the Bantu groups were forced to migrate again. However, with such powerful empires in place and such strong homesteads, migration was difficult. Battles over land ownership were more fathomable than the prospects of migrating and having to convert to a hunter-gatherer lifestyle. And so began a raging war between the Dingiswayo, Zwide, and Swazi Kingdoms.

All conflicts between these three kingdoms might have been resolved more peacefully if the respective chiefs had desired to distribute what was left of the land evenly. This wasn't the case, and each chief had his own agenda to acquire more land and civilians than his comrades. Their dreams and aspirations outweighed their ties of kinship. A wife was not worth the prospect of everlasting fame.

The Zwide had thousands more people under their rule than the Ngwane had and thus, their army was ten times larger.

Sobhuza was left with a choice. Would he fight, knowing he and his kingdom would succumb to the forces of his enemies? Or would he give the Ndwandwe people what they wanted?

Sobhuza figured that the defeat of his people would be too high a price to pay for any battle and took a small sample of his following and left Swaziland. Those he left behind, acknowledged and accepted their place within the Zwide Kingdom. Even Sobhuza's brother restrained his reservations towards the new leadership.

One might have thought that King Sobhuza would have felt ashamed that the very beginning of his career had been met with his cowardly retreat. Instead, he was a man of incredible resilience and bravery. He didn't hide his face in shame. He handled his defeat with wisdom and pose. Following his retreat, he created a second kingdom.

His neighboring chiefdoms saw this and were drawn to his recovery, paying him tribute and creating alliances with him. This encouraged him to attempt to reclaim his homeland. He gathered a small force from his own followers and his alliances and moved toward the Dlomodlomo hills in the hopes of conquering more land and harnessing more allies.

Along the way, he and his people accidentally stumbled into the uncharted lands of the Sotho people, who kidnapped and imprisoned Sobhuza and his followers for many days.

That was until Sobhuza's charm won the alliance of the Sotho Chief, who eventually released Sobhuza and his people.

While Sobhuza was talking his way out of a difficult predicament and forming an unlikely friendship, Zwide's grasp on Sobhuza's lost kingdom was waning.

The Dingiswayo had started to attack the Zwide claimed lands more frequently, and Zwide had finally formed a plan to retaliate. He decided that he would take his warriors, and together, they would cross the Mahlatsi river and surprise their enemies on the other side, sending them to their tombs.

Zwide's plan may have worked if someone had not told the Dingiswayo chief of it. As Zwide and his warriors were crossing the river, the Dingiswayo warriors were waiting and with great accuracy threw their spears at Zwide and his force. Zwide and a few others managed to escape with a cowardly retreat. His life had been saved, but he had lost his empire.

As soon as Zwide ran, so too had Sobhuza's brother sent word to Sobhuza, begging him to come home and reclaim the land that would now be claimed by the Dingiswayo.

Along his route to reclaiming his kingdom, Sobhuza and his allies married many more daughters of great chiefs and had brave sons with them. Sobhuza's reign and control over the African lands grew until, eventually, he found himself in control of a large enough force that could enable him to reclaim his home.

As for the citizens of Sobhuza's lost kingdom, they had heard the tales of his growing greatness as well as his intentions to reclaim his kingdom. Now that Sobhuza had become so renowned, he was redeemed in the eyes of the people he had lost to Zwide's warriors so long ago.

While the respect for Sobhuza grew within his lost kingdom, the Dingiswayo chief felt it transgressive to fight against Sobhuza and his growing force over land that was so small in comparison to what he already had control over. Dingiswayo rallied his troops and left

Sobhuza's old home, allowing the redeemed chief to step back into the borders of his once lost kingdom.

Sobhuza reclaimed his kingdom without bloodshed and when he did, the locals responded positively, paying tribute to him as their king.

As for the Dinganiswayo chief that had so kindly stepped aside, Sobhuza gave him two of his daughters to wed as a gift and an affirmation of peace. The two eventually became good friends (Gillis, 1999).

Spiritual Beliefs

The ancient Ngwane believed in a higher power called Mkhulumqanda. Mkhulumqanda created the earth and asked for nothing—no worship and no sacrifice in return. Mkhulumqanda is often very distant from the people and difficult to reach. Luckily, the women and the children of the tribe can see the ancestral spirits and ask them for guidance in the occasions that Mkhulumqanda's attention is needed but can't be obtained. It is the responsibility of the Swazi queen to make regular contact with the ancestral spirits to evoke the rains.

These ancestral spirits may appear to the queen and other women as ghosts, in dreams, or as snakes.

In the Swazi community, the *inyanga* and *tinyanga* are the healers of the group and the two people most closely associated with the spirits in the form of illnesses. The *inyanga*, using bone throwing methods, determines the ailment of the individual and suggests a prognosis. The *tinyanga* will then prepare a ritual and a herbal remedy that will alleviate the symptoms and or cure the patient.

The Swazis believe that everything around them is connected, and they work heavily with witchcraft and supernatural methods. On occasion, when a patient's illness is very serious, they may suggest human sacrifice as a means to a cure.

Along with the tribal healers is the *sangoma* who communicates with the spirits by allowing them to enter their own bodies. A *sangoma* is not a path that one can choose, rather it is a path that is chosen for you, a gift—or a curse, granted by the ancestors.

The powers of the young *sangoma* won't start to show until later on in life, and when they do, a choice needs to be made as to whether the individual wishes to pursue their gift. If they pursue it and do what they are destined for, they will live, but they must live their lives through the voices and words of their ancestors by allowing them into their own bodies. If they choose to refuse this gift, in a few months, they will die.

Culture

The Ngwane followed a hierarchical system based on the relationship clans had with the king and Queen.

The King and his wife were at the top of the pack, while their close friends and family, known as the King Bearers, were second from the top. Anyone who was not on a first-name basis with the King was placed at the bottom.

Once boys and girls reached a certain age, their families would begin to arrange marriages based on their place in society. Once the marriage was arranged, the husband would pay la bola for the bride in the form of cattle. A matrimony ceremony would be held, and the bride would then leave her clan to go and live with her husband's family until she became pregnant with their first child. By that point, the husband and wife would leave to build their own hut.

If the family was wealthy enough, the husband may arrange for a second wife. During the ceremony, the two women would be expected to look at each other and exchange vows as they accepted one another into their lives.

In some instances, the first wife would have majority control over the household happenings. However, should the second wife have a closer relationship with the king or the royal family, then she would take on the role of the first wife.

Within the city, the men were required to hunt and take care of the cattle, go to war and train the young boy in these areas while the women's roles were to maintain the resources of the house, care for the children, and harvest foods from the fields.

When a person dies, they are buried in the ground, however, if that person is of royalty, they are buried within a cave. The Swazi believe that once a person dies, they will come back in the form of an ancestor.

Folktales

The Flying Tortoise

The parrot flew down from the sky and landed on a branch beside her friend.

"Did you hear the news?" she asked.

"No," answered the bird.

"The cloud people have seen our drought and want to invite us all to a great feast so that we can eat," the parrot said.

"How kind of them."

The birds were the only creatures allowed to see the cloud gods.

The tortoise listening in on their conversation cried, "take me with you, I am starving."

"We can take you if you can fly," answered the birds.

"I can't fly," replied the tortoise.

"Well then, we can't take you with us."

"Please, I'll try anything," begged the tortoise.

And so the birds decided to help him. They went around gathering the feathers from all the other birds who had been invited to the feast.

The tortoise looked a little funny, but the idea worked,

and he started to float. With a little practice, the tortoise flew with the birds up into the sky to meet the cloud gods for a feast.

"What will we tell them?" said the bird to the parrot. "They'll ask why he looks like this."

"We'll say he is the God of Everyone," suggested the parrot.

"Yes, yes, I like that. I am the God of Everyone, and my name is everyone!" Shouted the Tortoise, and they all agreed.

When they got to the feast, none of the winged creatures could believe how much food the cloud gods had prepared.

"Thank you for coming, everyone may now eat," they said.

And Tortoise lifted his head and ate everything, while the other birds could eat nothing.

The birds were so angry that they all took back their feathers.

"Please, don't leave me here like this. I need to get home and I can't fly. I will have to jump, please leave me one feather?" begged the tortoise.

But none of the birds did.

The tortoise jumped and broke his shell on the rocks and from that day forth, whenever everyone sees the tortoise's shell, they remember what the cost of selfishness is.

This is a beautifully poetic tale that outlines the peaceful nature of the Swazi people (Hayzed, n.d.).

CHAPTER 9
KHOISAN AND THE PORTUGUESE

After having received word from the Arabs of a faster channel to India, the Portuguese started on their mission back from India and around the west African coast. When they arrived in the cape, they left their ship on boats and came to shore. Seeing life ripe and wealthy before them, they seized the women and the cattle they could and headed back to the ships.

The Khoisan men didn't hesitate to grab their weapons and with deadly accuracy shot the Portuguese thieves down with stones and poisoned arrows.

The survivors who managed to escape would be back for revenge for those who weren't and perished at the hands of the locals.

Three years later, as anticipated, the Portuguese came

back and asked the Khoisan to help them unload a gift for them and their people. They handed the Khoisan an assemblage of ropes and had them lug the ship, and its prize closer to shore. Once all the Khoisan were lined up, and the ship was yet to reach the shallows, the Portuguese pulled out a cannon, lit the gunpowder, fired, and left.

Thus was the legacy they left upon the locals.

Over time, the Portuguese would come to dominate the trades of the helpful Arabs by destroying the routes and the ports the group had created, leaving many of them stranded and forcing further group combinations in Africa to take place that would inevitably lead to the Sudanese and Ethiopian empires in later years.

Hungry for more, the Portuguese became swept up in Africa's resources and, where trade wasn't possible, didn't hesitate to take slaves and raid lands for themselves.

Their ambitions led them to the Monomotapa Empire, where they noticed the squirming for power between the chieftains. The King at the time was tired and ill from all the interclan fighting. The Portuguese took advantage and slaughtered him and his followers, taking as many survivors as they could to sell as slaves. Thus, the Portuguese conquered the Monomotapa Empire.

The Portuguese continued to use the Kingdom of Sofala after their victory as a trading center until they conquered Mozambique, then the old dynasty became nothing but an old outpost.

CHAPTER 10
THE KINGDOM OF ZWIDE

A History of the Ndwandwe People

Zwide first began to rule over his people in the Kingdom of Zwide during a challenging and dark time. The heat brought on by climate change had dried the rains and the lakes, leaving his people thirsty and their cattle dead. The little rain that they did get was quickly sucked up by their dominant farming grain, the mielie. There was little to eat, his people had begun to starve and he was growing poor. It was a desperate time, not one for friends.

During this time, the two biggest Kingdoms in the area were Zwide and Dingiswayo. The Kingdom of Swaziland was massively small in comparison and of no significance to King Zwide.

He didn't think that it would be possible for such a

small group to become such a big problem for him, not in the beginning at least.

And so, Ndinginisiwayo and Zwide began fighting over what remained of the river that separated them. There was one problem, Zwide's friends, the Swazi, lived right in the center of the battlefield.

In the midst of repelling and toying with the enemy whenever they came to the lake for a drink, the Zwide would fire arrows from their bows. The Dingiswayo citizens would run away and then bring back their army to retaliate, and the Swazi would, more often than not, get caught in the crossfire.

In 1817, en route to attack the Dingiswayo, they were ambushed while crossing lake Mhlatsi. King Zwide barely managed to escape (*Chief Dingiswayo*. n.d.).

Zwide ran as far south as he could, swearing revenge on the man who had taken everything from him.

Along the way, he and his followers met a white man on horseback. Although Zwide was unable to speak the man's language, he was able to identify that the man was on his way to the southern coast. Zwide and his followers walked with the man for some time and became increasingly anxious about him and the silver weapon he held in his belt. Zwide plotted to kill the man, in anticipation of conflict. Zwide reached for his spear, and as he did, the man pulled out his gun and shot, two times in the air, warning the people to stay back.

One of Zwide's men was able to spear the man from behind. The blade entered his heart and he fell off his horse and died.

That night, Zwide and his followers ate the horse and discussed the use of the strange metal weapon, and decided to use it to strike fear into the hearts of the smaller tribes that they might pass, and force them to join their group.

The next day, they continued south toward the coast, anticipating that there might be more of the white men there. As they went, they shot the white man's gun into the air, and nearly all the tribes they passed pledged their allegiance. Once again, his following had begun to grow.

Once they arrived at the southern coast, they met with the Portuguese, who had just finished a trip to the Asian trading dock. They were celebrating, having finally found the fastest route to the trade center and, had happened upon this new land.

Zwide and his people, seeing the spices, clothes, and seeds that the Portuguese had, decided to trade their cattle and their copper for the items in the hopes of ending their starvation and increasing their numbers.

Zwide's following grew, as did his relationship with the Portuguese.

Zwide told the Portuguese traders of his woes as they settled beside each other for a little while in the cape. The Portuguese analyzed his warriors before suggesting a few remedies to keep his warriors strong.

The recent circumcision of his warriors had been leaving them weak and pained. The warriors needed to be strong in mind and body. The grazing off of a piece of skin was leading them to failure.

Zwide agreed to stop the cutting at once.

The Portuguese trader further taught and trained Zwide and his warriors in battle, helping them correct their stances and enhance their stamina.

When Zwide left the Cape to return home, he knew he would exact his revenge on Dingiswayo, and he was right.

He returned home to find his land had been claimed by Dingiswayo and his new apprentice, Shaka Zulu. Without much warning or introduction, Zwide and his new followers attacked the unsuspecting tribe and kidnapped the chief. They took their prisoner back to their reclaimed lands and executed him.

Zwide's wife, Queen Ntombazi, a beloved *sangoma*, placed the ex-chief's head on a stick for all to see.

For Zwide, the plight against the Dingiswayo was over.

If only he had known that by ending one war, he would subsequently start another.

His victory was not enough for him, and he went on to destroy the Khumalo nation. The Khumalo nation had been formed under the dreaded Sotho-Tswana people, who had settled at their place of origin along the eastern coast. He murdered the royal family—everyone except the king Mzilikazi Khumalo, who managed to escape. Mzilikazi fled to the Zulu Kingdom where he met with Shaka to tell him of his encounter with Zwide.

Zwide's battle strategies had been relayed to his greatest enemy and placed him in a very vulnerable position.

And so the battle of Gqokli Hill began.

Zwide came with his forces to greet his rival. What he did not expect was for Shaka Zulu to have his own warriors, the Dingiswayo, and what was left of the Khumalo people on his side.

Still, Zwide and his people had been trained by the Portuguese, and there was little that could frighten them.

The groups slashed at each other, coating the ground in blood. Zwide and Shaka fought head to head with blood-curdling screams and hateful teeth gritting. Zwide ducked left while Shaka swung right, and while Shaka's head was turned, Zwide struck him with his spear.

Shaka's face reddened in anger. He was not a king who would die avenging someone he loved.

With a mighty battle cry, he spoke words of encouragement to his fellow warriors. He thrashed and lunged at Zwide, who was bewildered by this transformation into a dying man.

As Shaka's cries grew, so too did his troops' energy. One by one, the Zwide soldiers' throats were cut, and their bodies were impaled. Zwide, as he always did in the face of defeat, ran.

He ran to his once allied brother-in-law, Sobhuza. Zwide didn't know that Sobhuza was in cohorts with Shaka. Still fairly loyal to his brother-in-law, Sobhuza warned Zwide, and so Zwide carried on north, knowing that if stopped, he would be caught.

The warriors weren't people of polite and empty conversation. They skinned and burned the people of neighboring tribes to strike fear into their hearts and draw out the prisoner they sought (Bryant, 2010).

Finally, Zwide arrived in Tonga country, where he was given a final meal by the chief.

It wasn't long before Shaka's warriors showed up and executed him.

His wife, family, and all the people that lived within his borders were killed and had their ears and limbs chopped off and burned by Shaka's warriors.

Zwide's only living legacy was Swazi, protected by her loving Sobhuza (Maringozen, 2022).

Spiritual Beliefs

The Ndwandwe, Mthethwa, and the Zulus believed that there was a mystical land called Uthlanga. In this land grew a huge tree. One day, a seed from the tree dropped to the ground and sprouted a reed. This reed was Unkulunkulu, the god who would create every man, woman, creature, and child.

He would accomplish this upon the day that he grew too big for his stems. He shed his leaves and walked through the mystical garden, where he found other people growing in the reeds. He plucked them out, one by one. Then he found a special herb garden where he plucked out the medicine man and his dreams. He walked farther to a drier area where he plucked cattle, lions, lizards, and birds for his people to watch and eat.

Once every plant from the garden was harvested, he realized that the garden would not be big enough for his creations to enjoy. So, he grew mountains, plains, rivers, and oceans and sent his people out into the world.

One day, he decided to leave his beloved garden to visit his people, but he found that they were starving and tired. He taught them how to hunt, how to build fires, how to fish, and how to make medicine. Once the people understood and had remedied their health, he gave them and all the animals and plants names.

He watched his people work and dance and decided to send a message to them.

'You will live forever."

He gave the message to a lizard to deliver to the people.

But the Lizard was slow and Unkulunkulu grew impatient, thinking his people had abandoned him. Angered, he wrote another message.

'Death to all.'

He gave this to a faster lizard, wanting his people to know that they had angered him.

The faster lizard happened to pass the slow lizard on its way and, got to the people first.

Thus, people are not immortal beings.

It is believed that when a person is made up of a body, a life force, a shadow or darkness, and a spirit or soul. Each of these is a separate entity that works for its own purposes.

So when a man dies, his life force exits his body. If he has had a negative impact on those around him and has not completed his life's mission, his soul will fade away, and he will fade into the darkness to become a burden or a curse upon his family. But if he has had a positive impact on those around him and has fulfilled his goals in life, his shadow will disappear, and he will live again as an ancestor.

Culture

The Mthethwa, Dwandwe, and Zulus are exceptionally creative people. Music and dance make up a good proportion of their daily lives. Often at work, the women may sing songs to pass the time. The men may write poems or tell folktales about their legacy, dynasty, and chiefs. Their evening entertainment often consists of singing and dancing along to past battles performed by clan members while drinking pure, traditional African beer.

When they are not entertaining themselves with their cultural activities, the men are out hunting or training as warriors. The royals discuss political issues with their friends and confidants, but ultimately, they alone are the decision-makers, and they alone are responsible for their people's survival.

All fight training and hunting are first practiced with sticks. Boys from the age of three are given sticks to beat each other with. Every day, they use them and practice, sometimes with mentors and sometimes without. The boys become rapidly strong swordsmen and as they do, they also become more attractive to the women.

On the other hand, the women's jobs are to harvest and plant the crops, manage the resources, make the beer, and take care of household funds. Though women are usually not needed within the politics of everyday life, their voices are strongest and most decisive in their own households. For it is they who care for the children, educate the girls, and make sure the boys don't kill one another while their mentors are hunting. It is therefore the women who know best how to handle interclan conflict.

As the groups grew larger, sometimes too large for the chief to maintain regular control, policing systems were put into place, and the chief would send warriors out to ensure that rules and regulations were being followed. The warriors would use their keen eyesight and quick awareness to quickly find where treason was hidden, and where they couldn't do any monitoring themselves, they would gather spies and allies to help them.

These groups were polygamous, especially among the royals and wealthier groups. While in some cases, status was determined by how close one was to the chief, in other instances, status was determined by how much cattle, crops, and metal minerals one owned.

In the cases of marriages, most were arranged, though later on, marrying for love became more common. Once a marriage was arranged, a payment called *la bola* would be paid to the bride-to-be's father before the wedding day and the bride would move to live with the groom's family after.

In many ways, these groups borrowed cultural and societal ideologies from their neighbors. Most of them were acquired after the rise of the great and powerful Shaka Zulu

Folktales
Why the Cheetah Has Tear Stains

Once there was a very lazy hunter. He sat in the cool morning watching a group of springbuck grazing on the grass.

How nice it would be to have some fresh meat and not

have to do any of the work, he thought.

Suddenly he noticed something moving in the long grass. It was a cheetah. The cheetah was crouched low, seeking out a small springbuck. When the Cheetah was ready, she lurched and caught the springbuck. She then began to drag the meat back with her.

The hunter followed.

She carried the meat toward her den, where there were three cheetah pups.

How easy it would be to have a leopard do my hunting for me, thought the hunter.

And so he waited for the cheetah to leave before he went to the den and took all three pups.

When the Cheetah came back, she cried so loud that an old witch doctor walking past heard her. As the witch doctor learned of everything, he became very angry that the hunter had stolen the cheetah's pups, so he went to the village where he told the villagers the same thing. The villagers, too, were angry. So they all went to the hunter and kicked him out, rescuing the Cheetah's pups.

The old man gave the cheetah back her pups, and she was very happy.

The moral of this Zulu story is that one should always treat the immediate environment with care and respect. One must also always hunt using their skills, and they must not be lazy (Zulu Folk Tales, n.d.).

Khoisan and the Dutch

During this time, the Dutch had entered the cape for the first time, wrecking their ship along the rocks. The shipwrecked men found sanctuary on the shores of Africa. These would become the first white people to inhabit the cape. After several months there, the group was finally able to return home on a Portuguese ship, where they explained the benefits of moving a colony to Africa. Not long after, Van Riebeck and his group of vessels came to do just that.

Their first encounter with the Khoisan was peaceful and resulted in an immediate trading post.

All seemed to go smoothly between the newcomers and the locals. Except that, very quickly, the Dutch's belongings began to go missing. Their slaves would disappear and be found hiding among the local tribes, and their cattle and their gardens would be depleted upon their coming home.

In revenge, the newcomers would take the Khoisan people and force them into slavery. The Dutch would butcher Khoisan clans and take their livestock.

The Khoisan would subsequently retaliate.

The relationship between the two deteriorated very quickly, and it wasn't long before the Dutch Embassy sent orders to Van Riebeck to remove the locals from their homes, and he complied.

Once the locals retreated, it wouldn't be long before the Khoisan and the Xhosa would meet and combine forces to defeat the Dutch on several occasions.

CHAPTER 11
ZULULAND

A History

A young Senzagakhona was enjoying his days as King of the Zulus after his ancestor Malendellela had rebelled against his father, who had been the Chief of the Mthethwa people. Senzagakhona was a bit of a ladies' man, but even more so, he was a good chief.

One day, Nandi, a woman from one of his clans, proclaimed him to be the father of her child, whom she named Shaka, meaning beetle. He rejected the woman and denied the affair. Nandi and Shaka returned to their home, where they were also rejected on account of the chief. Nandi and Shaka left and wandered from tribe to tribe, trying to find a place to call home.

What man would love a woman shunned by the king? Who would marry her or even agree to?

Finally, as if the Unkulunkulu had a strange sense of humor, the mother and child found refuge with the Mthethwa people under Dingiswayo.

The chief of the Mthethwa was an expert warrior and a man hungry with ambition. He had his own ideas about warfare that had never before been attempted until his reign. He began to select his men carefully and then train them explicitly for combat.

One day, a leopard was seen sneaking into the cattle *kraal*. While the city folk ran for help and screamed for mercy, Shaka, who was eager to join the ranks of the warriors, single-handedly killed the leopard using nothing but his spear. While the beast leaped on him, he stabbed it through the heart.

This event gave him an idea. While he watched the Mthethwa warriors practice fighting by throwing spears back and forth every day, Shaka wondered what battles would be like if your opponent couldn't throw your own spear back at you.

He set off to design a new spear that could be used in the same way he had used to kill the leopard. He fastened a sharper and longer blade to a stick and called his intriguing invention the *iklwa*.

Dingiswayo hadn't been so ignorant as to not have noticed the boy's skills. After all, Shaka was the strange child who had offended his cousin. Dingiswayo had been keeping watch over the boy for a while, and with tension picking up among surrounding tribes, now was a good time to invest in the boy's skills.

Shaka joined the ranks and fought alongside the Dingiswayo warriors, and they defeated the Buthelezi, a neighboring Zulu tribe. Shaka had performed so well that he was immediately promoted. Following Dingiswayo's first defeat of the Ndwandwe and King Zwide, Shaka was given the rank of commander.

During their time together, Dingiswayo not only looked at Shaka as a student, but he began to see him as a son, wanting what was best for him and wanting to see him reach his goals and aspire to greatness that he was capable of.

Dingiswayo had defeated Ndwandwe and wanted to call a truce with his cousin, Chief Senzagakhona of the Zulus. The two met and made amends, and Dingiswayo managed to convince Senzangakhona that Shaka was indeed his son. Finally, after a number of repeated meetings, Dingiswayo had secured Shaka's future: Senzagakhona had agreed to let Shaka rule as the next King of the Zulus after his death.

All would have been well if Senzagakhona had kept his promise, but he didn't. Instead, his eldest established son claimed the throne.

Devastated by the betrayal, Shaka could not be consoled.

Though no one knows why or how it happened, but, the new king was quickly assassinated.

Could Shaka have been behind it?

Though that still remains a mystery, Shaka and his mother took the throne, he as the new Zulu king and she, as the queen mother.

The two people who had once been shunned so intolerably had finally risen above all those who had shamed them.

Though he still held close ties with the Dingiswayo dynasty, Shaka began to build an independent military empire. Every man within his walls was trained in how to use the *iklwa*, and in time, Shaka had a group of 500 sharply trained men.

Still harboring the hate from his childhood, Shaka sent his warriors out to his mother's home tribe that had rejected them so many years ago. The warriors struck down civilians and children while Shaka and his mother smiled as they burnt the perpetrators of their pain.

This ferocious killing of all creatures without regard of age or gender made Shaka and his warriors one of the most feared groups in Africa.

All for Shaka had now been amended. He was content with his mentor and humbled by his mother. Everything was fine until the day Chief Zwide executed Dingiswayo and had his head placed on a stick.

Shaka's world went red, and he sought redemption and fiery revenge on Chief Zwide. Wherever the betrayer went, Shaka would find him.

Luckily for Shaka, he wasn't the only one who harbored hate for the Ndwandwe chief. Soon, Mzilikazi Khumalo approached him after Mzilikazi's home had been invaded and his family slaughtered. Together, along with what was left of the Mthethwa people, they banded together to fight against Zwide.

During the battle, Shaka was wounded, and though his troops were victorious, Zwide had escaped.

Determined to find him, Shaka sent his warriors out to look for Zwide with the instruction to torture and kill anyone who got in the way. Shortly after, Shaka's warriors brought back rumors that the King of Swaziland, Sobhuza, had been harboring Zwide.

Shaka, acknowledging that Sobhuza had never once harmed him and could be as hateful of Zwide as he was given the history, decided to make the man an offer he couldn't refuse. He would give Sobhuza a new wife and form an alliance with him, or if his gift was rejected, he would find a reason to get Sobhuza executed.

Sabhuza agreed but warned his brother-in-law about the danger ahead.

The warriors marched on, and no one has given mercy, not even the people of Swaziland.

They chopped limbs from bodies and ears from heads. They burned skin until it was crispier than burnt corn until, finally, they were able to track Zwide to a *kraal* in Tonga and executed him.

Many of the groups that had been tortured along the way had been forced under the control of Shaka and his Kingdom. Shaka had become drunk with power. He could have 50,000 men fighting for him for whatever he wanted at any given moment.

Then, in 1825, the British entered Africa (Flank, 2015). Their paths of destruction had been reported all over. Shaka had heard the news and feared what might happen if he was not on good terms with these strange people. He sent a group of his warriors down to the Cape to commence trading with them and cordially invited them to his lands.

Shaka had always been an eloquent speaker and a fast learner. Somehow, he was able to meet the British colonizers halfway and gave them the land and the people of Natal to do with as they pleased.

A few years later, Shaka's mother died of illness. Shaka was unbelievably devastated. Already suffering from mood swings and bouts of rage, he further lost his mind upon her death. As he mourned her, he forced his people to mourn her too. No crops were allowed to be grown or harvested, no meat was allowed to be hunted, no fish could be caught, and no celebrations were to take place. Anyone who broke the rules was punished immeasurably.

The people looked on at their once proud and heroic king in horror and pain. Their support waned, and the land trembled as the groups decided to start pulling away.

Something had to be done to protect such a great and pivotal empire.

Shaka's two half brothers, established sons of Senzangakhona, formed a pact and killed him.

As he lay dying in their arms, Shaka reportedly asked them to bury him in a tomb.

Thus ended the legacy that was Shaka Zulu's (Flank, L. 2015).

Khoisan and the British

After the war with Napoleon, Britain was a depleted nation. In desperate need of resources, they sent out valued members to colonize Africa. The group arrived on the coast of Port Elizabeth, where they moved further inland and began to establish towns around the Eastern Cape.

When the British arrived, the Dutch, the Xhosa, the Khoisan, and the Korana were already at war and had been for years. Siding with the Dutch, the British got involved and managed to hinder the Xhosa's movements into the coastal lands.

Meanwhile, both British and Dutch Missionaries had delved further inland toward the Zulu Kingdom in the hopes of converting the warriors to Christianity.

The rapid growth of the British colonies within the

African coastal regions had chiefs rallying to catch their attention in an attempt to form a relationship that would protect them and their people from the tightening of colonist influence on the people. The African chiefs offered land, which led to a miscommunication in which the white settlers thought that anyone in Africa could offer land because to the British, land was wealth and wealth was property.

Once the lands promised had been seized, they would be taken again by a neighboring tribe or the tribe that sold it to them in the first place. This misunderstanding angered the colonists, who were quick to anger and ready to solve their problems.

Thus, without bargaining, the British, the Dutch, and various other parties began to seize the land of Africa, its peoples, and its ghosts as their own.

CHAPTER 12
THE HOUSE OF MPONDO

A History

After his father was killed in a war between the Bomvana and the Mpondo, Faku Ngqungqushe's brother was to claim the throne. But this didn't happen.

In Ancient Mpondo society, polygamy was a viable and customary way of life. Faku's father had married twelve wives and had over 20 sons. Traditionally, it is the first son of the first wife who will become the King's predecessor once he passes. If this doesn't happen, the second eldest son in the family is given the title.

None of this happened. Faku's mother was one of the later wives, and it was perceived that upon his birth, Faku would never have the title of chief.

However, when the time came for the new chief to rise,

the council that advised and guided the chief found that none of the wives, except for one, was good, kindhearted, or eloquent enough to produce an heir that would sustain and grow the people.

After visiting their separate homes and dining with each of the wives, it was certain. The true mother of the people needed to be someone who could see a dispute from more than one side. She had to see people for who they were and discern how they felt without asking. She had to be smart—but not too smart—and giving—but not without hesitation. Most of all, she had to have sway over the previous king and the people. She had to speak so well that she made even deaf men hear. This was the mother of Faku.

Thus, Faku claimed the throne, unprepared and virtually illegitimate but very brave.

Tension swarmed throughout the family. Brothers swore against brothers as they tried to find peace with the decision of the Council, but as none of them were on the Council and as none of them were King, their concerns fell on deaf ears.

Faku's brother, Phakani, who was supposed to have been the late Ngqungqushe's predecessor left the tribe with his mother where they settled among the Hintsa Gcaleka, a Mpondo clan, hating Faku and his legacy from afar.

Though his other brothers remained, the resentment in the house was strong for some time. The elder brothers,

AFRICAN HISTORY

Mtengwana and Gambushe, who were also close in line for the throne, were very angry with the outcome. Some sources claim that Faku and his two brothers went to war within the house, fighting one another with sticks to spears, hoping one another dead.

Eventually, Mtengwana settled with the Bomvana, the betrayers that had gone to war with his own tribe only a few months ago and killed his father.

Gambushe felt his presence would stir Faku into a frenzy that would inevitably lead to the younger brother's end, so Gambushe stayed and hoped that this would be the case.

Along with his family splitting apart to create tribes that wished for his end, Faku's beginnings were littered with threats from the surrounding Zulu influences and what would become known as the Mfecane wars—the battles between the Ndwandwe, Mthethwa, and the Zulu.

He didn't have much time to consider his new position before King Senzagakhona, Shaka Zulu's father, attacked his small home and its people in the Transkei. So quickly did the young King lose everything: his cattle, his family, and his friends.

The people saw Faku as a failure and ran to the Xesibe Chief of another Mpondo clan, begging for a new beginning, but the chief refused. One of his daughters had been married to the late Mpondo King, and he decided to keep his word to his late friend and ensure that the Mpondo clan remained sturdy. Threatening the people who had asked for sanctuary, the chief sent them all back.

With his people returning and his end nearing, Faku had to find a way to win back the respect of those who had rejected him. So he decided to start by seeking revenge on his father's killers, the Bomvana, now his brother Mtengwana's people.

This goal created further tension between Faku and his brother Gambushe, who had stayed. Faku rose three ranks, claimed himself as the rightful chief, and forced Gamushe and his followers to help him. Reluctantly, Gambushe agreed. Together, they raided the lands around them, moving through Hintsa Gcaleka kingdom, where Phakani and his mother had settled. They continued to be victorious, claiming back all the groups that had rejected Faku's legacy.

The Bomvana, with a new enemy and a chief with years of experience, set out a counterattack that forced Faku's men to flee, returning home, again, with nothing.

Gambushe was at his wit's end. His brother had tried to convince him that he was the king the people needed, but Gambushe couldn't see it. He stayed on the battlefield with his followers, never to return home.

Alone, with no one to console him, Faku was humiliated.

What he did not know was that though his brothers

laughed at his position and his ideas, his enemies, the old Bomvana chief, and the Zulu king, were aware of his potential and were slowly trying to move their captured groups away from his home in case, his true glory finally came to pass.

It did, but not in the manner that one might imagine for a Chief in wartime.

As the years went by, Faku learned that the Portuguese settlers in Africa had increased and that many of these settlers were now raiding or purchasing groups of Africans of varying ethnicities to be slaves in the growing economies of the world. This led ancient Bantu groups such as the Korana, who had so long ago shoved the Khoi toward the Cape, to work alongside the invaders in return for their own protection by raiding kingdoms and capturing slaves, which they would deliver unto the clutches of the tradesmen in the Cape. Guns and horses flowed as thick as the blood in the rivers. The British colonizers, too, were settling in rather nicely and forming their own trading ports and alliances among the people. Christianity was growing as the British ministers made their way through the kingdoms, forming alliances with chiefs and subsequently setting up posts in nearby villages. Catholicism was growing through the influence of the Portuguese, and the Dutch were seizing control over the now transformed Khoisan lands. Along with the political influences of the new company, the climate was now much hotter. Crops were dying and draining the water supply. The agricultural trade with the

Europeans, although economically and financially beneficial and creating rapid growth in cities, was, in many ways, causing an equally rapid environmental collapse. The land wasn't so fertile anymore, and the cattle were starving.

All these happenings played on the new King's mind. What was he to do?

He could, like the Hintsa Gcaleka chief and the Thembu people, form a relationship with William Shaw, a British minister, and allow the clergyman to take up a post outside the border and promote Christianity in return for his people's protection. He could also rebel against them as Khoisan had tried alongside the Xhosa. Alas, those groups had both failed in their endeavors to rid themselves of colonial influences.

What if he ignored the influences, and they came for him, seeking some kind of retribution? Would he not put his people at risk?

And what of the Zulus? What of Senzagakhona's expanding kingdom? What of this proclaimed son of his, Shaka Zulu? How was he to protect his people against the Zulu raiders? What if Shaka were to feud against his true father and raid their lands too?

Faku was known for being a thoughtful chief, always thinking and always pondering the best course of action.

After careful thought, he chose to let the Zulus pass

through his lands, and take what they would. After all, who of his people truly wanted to stay with him? Those who did could move closer inland, where it was safer. As for the ministers, he saw not a power among them great enough to protect him in the long run. The British, though, were an intriguing and quickly growing force, perhaps it would be best to form relationships with them.

At a crossroads, this is what the new Chief decided to do. He would stand in absolute solitude, a peacemaker among the chaos. He would make friends where he could, and leave those who called him an enemy to find resources in his land.

His choice proved to be a good one. Shaka's father, Senzakagakhona died, and Shaka became the new chief. Though there was never a feud between the relatives, Faku wasn't wrong in his assessment that blood would be spilled under Shaka's rise. Faku quickly established himself and his people as nonthreatening during the Zulu raids. This position caught Shaka's attention, and the two agreed that Faku's lands would not be disturbed so long as the routes within could be used by the Zulu Warriors on their excursions.

The minister's alliance with the Bomvana and the Thembu proved futile. When the Zulus attacked, the minister's prayers did little to save them, and the two groups were forced out of their home. Some survivors settled under the Zulu Kingdom, while the others tried to keep what was left of their histories and culture alive by seizing land from elsewhere. Faku's land would be elsewhere.

The Thembu attacked him, and he quickly repelled them, claiming his rule over the people.

More refugees settled on Mpondo lands, though most were from failed attempts at conquering Faku and his people.

Everything changed when the close allies of the Bomvana, the Tshomani, and the Baca, failed in their attempts to save their civilizations by conquering Faku's lands. Faku, not the greatest of warriors but a man who praised practice and thought above anything else, killed the Tshomani chief in battle, and his people's vision of him was forever changed.

The Bomvana chief knew that if he sided against Faku, he may suffer the same fate. He had put much thought into war and the conquering of lands, but he had not put protections in place, and his people were in danger. The Bomvana chief formed an alliance with Faku by offering him a wife—the Bomvana chief's daughter.

Faku could have laughed at the proposal and watched his lifelong enemy fall, but he didn't.

Faku bravely turned the other cheek and wed the girl, who birthed him a son who would become a greater fighter than even Shaka Zulu.

It would be his son, Ndamase, who would go on to conquer the lands that his father would rule and later pass on to him, even though he, too, was born too late to have a rightful claim to the throne among his brothers.

If Faku taught anything to his children, it was that leadership and respect are earned through lifelong hard work. It is not a gift, but a serious and difficult job (Stapleton, 2006).

Spiritual Beliefs

The Mpondo and Thembu both fall under the Xhosa cultural and spiritual lineage.

These groups believe in the higher powers of uThixooru and his son, uQamata.

Uthixoru, the sun god, created everything on the earth, from the trees to the creatures that roamed it. In his attempt to create his people, he created the first human, and the creator of the Xhosa people, uQamata, whom he claimed as his son. uQamata went out into the world as the first human and gave rise to the others. When he died, he rose again to take a seat alongside his father. uQamata's power was unlimited and unimaginable. He was so great, that it was believed dangerous and disrespectful to call upon him and disturb his peace.

Though their gods could not and were not regularly contacted, these people communicated regularly with their ancestors, spirits of chiefs, and people who had once lived among them. Sacrifices and rituals were performed on a daily basis to appease these spirits, who could either choose to favor them or destroy them. The ancestors commonly presented themselves in the form of dreams and to chosen ones in trances.

Animals were slaughtered to feed the onlooking spirits. Honey and beer were placed in specific holy shrines for the ancestors to enjoy, and water was given plenty.

The ancestors required warmth, food, and entertainment as much as the living did. But sometimes this was not enough to appease them. The ancestors regularly sought a voice to speak through to make demands and suggestions to the people. These announcements could have dire consequences if ignored or positive ramifications if heeded and followed through. Mostly, the decision was up to the individual, or in greater cases, the chief. Depending on the situation, there might be no way to appease the ancestors without being destroyed entirely by another entity or tribe.

People who were believed to have great understanding and influence over the ancestors were sorcerers, divination seekers, healers, and herbalists. These people could influence the ancestors' whims just as easily as the ancestors could influence theirs. A sorcerer who was angry at another could influence the ancestors by providing them with good food and a good reason to inflict illness on the offending party.

When a mother among these groups gives birth, she is required to seclude herself for ten days after giving birth so that the magic spawned by her enemies will not reach her child and destroy it. At the end of the ten days, an animal is sacrificed to appease the ancestors in the hope that they will leave the infant and mother alone permanently.

The position of diviner or sorcerer can come through either natural gifts or practice. If it's a gift, the person is merely a voice for the ancestors and isn't held responsible by the spirits for what events their messages may bring. If one practices sorcery and uses the ancestors, that person may be held accountable for their actions and those around them. They are susceptible to punishment by the spirits themselves. Practicing divination can be dark and dangerous, but it may bring glory to those who practice it well.

Herbalists and healers merely make sacrifices to the ancestors and ask for guidance in healing ailments, so they are not necessarily responsible for their messages but maybe if the ancestors so choose to use them.

Culture

The ancient culture of these people enforces the idea that men are powerful, intelligent rulers while women are intelligent and creative careers and, on most occasions, representatives of their ancestors. This belief is consistently displayed through evening entertainment such as dancing and singing. In these activities, the women will evoke the movements of their general responsibilities of caring for the children, protecting their families from evil, and conserving household resources. The men, on the other hand, evoke their memories of their battles and those of their ancestors. They display acts of hunting and leadership, and they pay tribute to the current chief by reciting poems.

The men were expected to be warriors in their own right, strong and wealthy. When a man wanted a bride, he was to kidnap her from her home and take her as his own before proceeding with the bridal payment. In cases where the marriage was arranged, it was still expected of him to take control and ownership over his bride, that way, she would learn to respect him and see the strength in his eyes as he would learn to nurture and cherish her with everything he had.

Polygamy was common in these cultures, with men often having more than three wives. The first wife would undoubtedly have full control over the household, including the other wives. Each of the wives and their respective children would be provided with their own hut and their own resources to feed their growing family. The husband would spend equal time with each of his wives but would expect the first wife to handle disputes without his assistance. Should a wife try to sway the perception of her husband against the other wives, she would be greatly disgraced within the family.

With regard to inheritance, the firstborn son would be given ownership over his father's resources and would be expected to continue to care for his brothers and his stepmothers as well as his own growing family.

In the event that the first son is not able to take over

the care of his family, the inheritance would be passed down to the next oldest son.

Until the time when the new carer was ready for marriage, his mother would take control of household duties. Once he became married, the task would be assigned to his first wife.

A man's family, which may range from about 20 to 100 individuals is considered a clan, and should the man become wealthy enough and renowned enough, he may enjoy an elite title or, if he finds difficulty in following the current chief, he may start a tribe of his own.

The chief is a man who holds massive influence over a number of people he can subsequently call his followers. One chief may rule over hundreds of thousands of clans, both rich and poor. The job of a chief is to ensure the protection, safety, and legacy of his people by going to war to obtain land and resources and by appeasing the spirits.

Folktales
Lion and the Jackal

Jackal was out hunting one day and noticed a bushbuck grazing not too far away. He looked at the bushbuck and sighed, for the buck was too big for him to catch and too heavy for him to take home to feed his family.

If only he had someone to help him catch it.

So he carried on and bumped into Lion.

"Say Lion, why don't you and I hunt together?" asked

Jackal.

The Lion agreed.

"That's fine, but if we catch something small, you get to take that to your family and if we catch something big, I can take that to my family."

Jackal agreed, and the two set off.

The first animal they came across was a big eland.

"This one is mine, go to my home and call my children to take the meat."

Jackal agreed and once Lion had gone he went and called his own children to take that meat.

"How can he think I'll bring this to his family while mine are starving?" Said Jackal.

Once Lion returned home, he turned to his wife.

"How was the meat?" "What meat?" she asked.

"Did Jackal not come and call my children to fetch the meat?" he asked.

"No," said his wife.

Lion was very angry and went to Jackal's home to confront him.

"Jackal, why did you not send for my children as I asked you to?" said Lion through the door.

But Jackal kept quiet and pretended not to be home.

The next day, Jackal got thirsty and made his way to the watering hole. Suddenly, he saw Lion's reflection in the water, so he ran and ran until he saw a little hole and flung himself in.

Lion was quick and caught Jackal's tail just in time.

"Ah, that's not my tail," said Jackal.

"Go and get a stone to smash at it with, and you'll see there is no blood."

And so Lion turned to find a stone to prove it really was Jackal's tail that he held, and when he looked back, Jackal had flung himself farther into the hole.

So Lion waited for him to come out, and Jackal lay in hiding hoping he would leave.

As the night set in and Jackal wanted to go home, he could see that the Lion was not in front of his hole waiting, but he was sure he was somewhere.

"Hello, my friend, It's me, I'm going to come out now," Jackal cried, and waited for a reply.

When none came, he scampered out of the hole and ran away.

Lion tried to catch him, but Jackal was too quick.

The next day, the Lion and Jackal had chosen to be friends again. They were hunting together when they came upon a small bushbuck.

"Here, take this thigh and go give it to my wife," said Lion, and Jackal took the thigh and gave it to his own wife.

When he returned, Lion handed him a shin. "Go and take this to your wife now," he said. Jackal took the shin to Lion's wife and upon his handing it to her, she said, "That's not mine," then Jackal slapped her with it and went back to Lion.

"Here, take this stomach to my wife," said Lion, and Jackal took the meat to his own wife.

When Lion got home, his wife was weeping and the children were scared.

"Why do you weep?" Lion asked her.

"How can you send Jackal to give me a shin and then to beat me?" she cried.

Lion was furious.

This is a tremendous tale that really explains the act of wisdom from systems of behavior and patterns (Story of the Hare, n.d.).

CHAPTER 13
THEMBULAND

A History

Chief Nxeko had three sons, Hlanga, Dlomo and Ndungwana. After he passed, his successor was to be Hlanga. However, after careful consideration by the council, it was decided that Hlanga did not have the qualities of a good, kindhearted, and open-minded leader. Knowing this, Dlomo, the second eldest, knew that he would have to prove himself to the council to be the leader they desired. He rallied support from the youngest brother, Ndungwana, who stood behind him as Dlomo challenged Hlanga to a stick battle for the position. Dlomo won and was proclaimed the new chief.

However, when Dlomo claimed the throne, many of the people revolted, for his position was not customary for a second-born son. These people chose to remain under Hlanga's leadership.

The late Nxeko's once united and proud nation had, in one fell swoop, been dismantled. Dlomo took those who would follow him and left, claiming lineage under a new name, the Hala.

Then there were those people who wished neither to follow Dlomo or Hlanga. These people were given to Ndungwana to rule over while pledging allegiance to victorious Hala. Ndunwana's people were titled Amandungwana.

Hlanga, despite his disposition, chose to pledge allegiance to Hala as well.

And so the Thembu nation was divided into three separate and quasi-independent kingdoms, and the people became as divided as the brothers. They worked together only out of spite and past promise.

The division got bigger over time as the Amathembu suffered falling-outs with allies and neighboring tribes, all of whom were scrambling to survive the attacks from the reigning Shaka Zulu.

Hala's wife gave birth to a son, Ukumkani, who would be the next ruler of the Amathembu.

Hala died in battle, and uKumkani was placed under a number of stresses his father had left for him to manage. In addition, the introduction of the British into Africa was plaguing uKumkani's mind and was a source of great dissatisfaction for him and his people. If the British were to attack them, his kingdom would divide further. Fearing the worst, he sought to build a relationship with the British missionaries and offered them a post.

His people were outraged, as were those in his uncles' territories. These people scrambled to find refuge under a king who would make wiser and more traditionally sound decisions. With the brothers giving support to the British, the people knew they would not find what they sought in Thembuland.

Word began to spread to the Gcaleka Hintsa, the greatest of the neighboring Xhosa nations, that Thembuland was ripe with civil unrest. The people and the chiefs were vulnerable and could be claimed under another.

The Gcaleka Hintsa attacked, taking over Amathembu little by little. They might have succeeded in claiming the entirety of the kingdom if it hadn't been for the new Cape Government having noticed the two groups' excursions along with the rest of the Mfecane fighting. The government claimed ownership over the two groups, hoping to dismantle them both.

Shaka Zulu also thought it wise to take advantage of the situation and claimed as many of the people as he could.

Then came along Madzicane of the amaBhaca, who also wanted a piece of these splintering tribes.

The survivors were afraid, alone, and bitter.

The people of Amathembuland now included a few descendants of the original tribe, hiding refugees, tortured enemies of the tribes around them, and lost clans trying to seek refuge.

uKumkani, like his father, died in battle while trying to reunite his people. His son, Bawana, wouldn't let the separation go on any longer. He decided to move the people east, out of where the Cape Government had placed them, and away from Shaka's growing army and any further threats.

If they were going to find peace as a nation and reunite as people, they needed to be secluded.

But their hopes changed to despair. They never made it to the sanctuary. Rumors of their move had spread back to the Cape Government, who sent men out to hinder and capture them.

Thembuland would never see the rejoining of its people (Mvene, 2020).

CHAPTER 14
XHOSALAND

A History

In Xhosaland, the position of the king was a little different from that of their neighboring tribes. A king did not rule over everyone. He, by birthright, is claimed to be the king, but his brothers, the junior chiefs, had the ability to do and say what they wanted. The king had no control over them. Each chief and king had their own group of counselors, who were the boys among their clans that had been sent on the day of the future chief's birth to work within their households. The counselors were advisors to the chiefs and would meet regularly to discuss disputes and how to better arrange the chieftains' placements within the land to avoid further conflict.

It was customary for the chief siblings to live a good

distance apart from one another.

During the 1800s, as Xhosaland grew, with its chieftains spreading out and its new inhabitants—the people they subsequently conquered, they met with the now combined Khoisan groups (Maringozen, 2022).

The chieftains of Xhosaland had, along their route toward the Cape, destroyed many of the Khoisan enemies and in so doing had formed uninitiated and unexpected allies. The Khoisan gave their services to the chiefs readily and in return, were granted positions of power, wives, and wealth.

The Xhosa people had been practicing agriculture for millennia. They were not hunters, nor were they gatherers. When it came to battle, they were ferocious but inaccurate in their archery.

The Khoisan, having the experience of master huntsmen combined with master herders, were very helpful in solving this problem and trustworthy when it came to keeping the Xhosa's cherished weapons.

The Khoisan found themselves in awe of the Xhosa power and were glad to have such strong protectors among them.

Once the Dutch began to settle along the coast, the groups were glad to be on familiar terms as they battled against the Dutch for farming space. The groups would encounter one another nine times on the frontier. Eventually, the Khoi would leave, unable to fight against such skilled gunmen.

During the Xhosa chief's reign, he was tasked with securing his people against Shaka's raids while trying to expand his land and following, as well as fending off the British and the Dutch alongside his brother chieftains, he grew tired.

One day, he was invited to a meeting with the British to discuss peace between their groups. He was too tired to ask his guards to accompany him. After refusing the British terms for peace, he was shot in the head.

Devastated, his brothers would continue to fight the white colonists until their last breath (Nomedz, 2022).

CONCLUSION

And so the colonizers surrounded the people, claiming them as their own. As for the people of Africa, they would be fighting back for many years to come. Even once colonization had run its course and was long gone, the Africans are still fighting, their ancestors still calling and their hopes unhindered. Though the world may see to it that their history isn't taught with the care that the history of other continents is, they know the truth. They were there, and they remember the tales told about men who spent hours every day looking up at the stars just to count how many steps west they had taken since they set off on a hunt. They remember the stories about the women who spent hours every day singing songs and braiding hair so that they might be able to do so with rapid speed and accuracy when they were married. These people remember the moments of greatness shared among family and friends when the celebrated spoke for days on the most magical passions of their existence.

Who are we to doubt them?

History Brought Alive takes you one step further into the past and places you right there besides these glorious figures in history because once you're there, once you see it, you will never forget it.

These have all been well-researched and accounted-for theories that are widely accepted as the possibilities of a fragmented and very blotchy puzzle. There are a thousand more accepted interpretations yet to be explored.

What if the truth was that Shaka never intended to save his people from the British Colonists?

What are the chances that the Mpondo king was being swayed by his council, who were more indebted to his mother than they were to him?

And what if the Portuguese never made any of their attacks or advancements of their own accord? What if it was their embassy all along telling them what to do?

While no view is more substantial or developed than another and all have their place, History Brought Alive places the interpretations of the original people and their feelings regarding their heroes above outside voices.

Because who would know better? There is no one.

History Brought Alive has been fact-checked by dozens of helpful writers and editors alike, only using the most recent and accepted sources and arguments from well-known and respected researchers and historians.

There is nothing more poetic out there than African History. It doesn't need a snappy title or a great romance because it is already full of great deeds and legends. Here we bid farewell to some of the greatest myths and legends that ever existed.

REFERENCES

African Pygmies: The world's shortest tribe. 2020. Hadithi. https://hadithi.africa/african-pygmies-the-worlds-shortest-tribe/

A Venda folktale. n.d. Tambani. http://tambani.co.za/venda-folktales/folktales-in-english/the-year-of-hunger-2/

Makaudze, G. 2013. It still makes sense!: Shona ngano (folktale) and the contemporary Zimbabwean socio-economic and cultural setup. *International Journal of development and sustainability*, 2(2), 521-529.

African Roots: The Nguni Tribe of Southern Africa. 2015. Genesis Magazine. https://genesismagz.com/southern-africas-largest-tribe-the-ngunis/

Ashton, N. 2013. *Rwanda in Focus*. Intercontinental Cry. https://intercontinentalcry.org/the-batwa-rwandas-invisible-people-19581/

Balyage, Y. 2000. *Ethnicity and Ethic Conflict in the Great Lakes Region*. Bugema University. https://opendocs.ids.ac.uk/opendocs/bitstream/handle/20.500.12413/4968/Balyage-MAK-Res.pdf?sequence=1

Batwa *people and experience*. 2021. Primate World Safaris. https://primateworldsafaris.com/the-batwa-people-experiences/

Batwa: The history and culture of a marginalized people in Central Africa. Unrepresented Nations and Peoples Organisation. https://unpo.org/article/19031

Beck, R. B. 2000. *The history of South Africa*. Greenwood Publishing Group.

Bewitched forests and waters of the VhaVenda (part 1). 2013. Van Hunks. http://www.vanhunks.com/lowveld1/venda1.html

Brian, F. 2005. *Tribal Warfare and "Ethnic Conflict" Cultural Survival*. https://www.newsweek.com/biologist-eo-wilson-why-humans-ants-need-tribe-64005

Bryant, A.T. 2010. *The Stabbing of Shaka and Ndwandwe War that Led to the Movement of The Ngoni and Others From Zululand*. Ngoni People.

https://www.ngonipeople.com/2010/10/stabbing-of-shaka-and-ndwandwe-war-that.html

Chabururuka, N. 2019. *Mwari the One God*. The Patriot. https://www.thepatriot.co.zw/feature/mwari-the-one-god/

Chacha. n.d. *What to Know About Zulu People, Their Culture and Tradition*. Answers Africa. https://answersafrica.com/what-to-know-about-the-zulu-people-their-culture-and-tradition.html

Choi, C. 2009. *The Final Days of Homo erectus*. Inside Science. https://www.insidescience.org/news/final-days-homo-erectus

Cief Dingiswayo. n.d. SA History. https://sahistory.org.za/people/chief-dingiswayo

Cirjak, A. 2020. *What Was The Original Name Of Africa?* World Atlas. https://www.worldatlas.com/articles/what-was-the-original-name-of-africa.html

Clemence, M., & Chimininge, U. 2015. Totem, Taboos and sacred places: An analysis of Karanga people's environmental conservation and management practices. *Int J Humanit Soc Sci Invent*, 14(11), 7-12.

DeBeer, J. n.d. *Camelthorn Giants*. Bushman Stories. http://www.bushmenstories.co.za/

Dunham, W. 2014. *Knuckle Sandwich: Did fFst Fights Drive Evolution of Human Face?* Reuters. https://www.reuters.com/article/us-science-face-idUSKBN0EK1OD20140609

Eric. 2021. *Pygmies Now an Endangered Hominid Species in Africa: Bantu Expansion Threatens Their Existence*. Human Evolution News. https://subspecieist.com/indigenous-tribes/pygmies-bantu/

Flank, L. 2015. *Shaka Zulu: The Real Story. Hidden Stories*. https://lflank.wordpress.com/2015/07/31/shaka-zulu-the-real-story/

Flemming, E. 2020. *What was pre-colonial Africa*. Sid Martin Bio. https://www.sidmartinbio.org/what-was-pre-colonial-africa

From Butwa to Mthwakazi: Celebrating history, culture. 2019. The Patriot. https://www.thepatriot.co.zw/old_posts/from-butwa-to-mthwakazi-celebrating-history-culture

Gee, H. 2021 *How Homo erectus Was, and Was Not, Like Modern-Day Humans.* Literary Hub. https://lithub.com/how-homo-erectus-was-and-was-not-like-modern-day-humans

Giama, C. 2016. *The Surprisingly sticky Tale of the Hadza and the Honey Guide Bird.* Atlas Obscura. https://www.atlasobscura.com/articles/the-surprisingly-sticky-tale-of-the-hadza-and-the-honeyguide-bird

Gillis, D. H. 1999. *The Kingdom of Swaziland: Studies in political history (No. 37).* Greenwood Publishing Group.

Guenther, M. G. 1999. *Tricksters and trancers: Bushman religion and society.* Indiana University Press.

Hadza social-organization. n.d. Exploring Africa. https://www.exploring-africa.com/en/tanzania/hadzabe/hadza-social-organisation

Hamilton, D. L. 1996. *The Mind of Mankind: Human Imagination, the Source of Mankind's Tremendous Power.* Suna Press. http://novan.info/ant.htm

Hayzed. n.d. *A Lesson for Everyone (Swaziland Folk Tale).* Quote. https://www.quotev.com/story/7654275/Folktales-around-the-world/10

Henderson, J, S. 1930. *The South-Eastern Bantu.* Cambridge University Press.

History of Great Zimbabwe. 2014. The Herald. https://www.herald.co.zw/history-of-great-zimbabwe/

Husseinali, N. 2013. *Hadza 4: Exploring the Lifestyle.* Word Press. https://moizhusein.wordpress.com/2013/01/02/hadza-4-exploring-the-lifestyle/

Ian. 2021. *Batwa "Pygmies": History and Present.* Experts Gorilla Highlands. https://experts.gorillahighlands.com/daily-dose/2021/05/17/batwa-pygmies-history-and-present

Jardin, X. 2009. *What Became of Neanderthals? We Ate 'em, Made 'em into Jewelry, Says Scientist.* Boing Boing. https://boingboing.net/2009/05/18/what-became-of-neand.html

Kora. n.d. SA History Online. https://www.sahistory.org.za/article/kora

Kwekudee. 2013. *Batwa People: One of the First People on Earth and the Original Inhabitants of Great Lakes Region in East Africa Before The Bantus Arrival. Trip Down Memory Lane.* https://kwekudee-tripdownmemorylane.blogspot.com/2013/03/batwa-people-one-of-first-people-on.html

Kwekudee. 2014. *Ewondo (Yaunde) People: The original Inhabitants of Yaounde, The Capital of Cameroon.* A Trip Down Memory Lane. https://kwekudee-tripdownmemorylane.blogspot.com/2014/09/ewondo-yaunde-people-original.html

Ladz. 2016. *How the Khoikhoi Society Was Organized Political Organization.* Mubula History. https://mubulahistory.blogspot.com/2016/12/how-khoikhoi-society-was-organized.html

Lederle, G. 2014. *Hunting with the Hadza.* Africa Geographic Stories.https://africageographic.com/stories/hunting-with-the-hadza

Lewis, J. 2002. *Forest hunter-gatherers and their world: a study of the Mbendjele Yaka pygmies of Congo-Brazzaville and their secular and religious activities and representations* (Doctoral dissertation, University of London).

Lewis-Williams, J. D. (2018). Three nineteenth-century Southern African San myths: a study in meaning. *Africa*, 88(1), 138-159.

Little, B. 2021. *How Did Humans Evolve? History.* https://www.history.com/news/humans-evolution-neanderthals-denisovans

Lutz, M. 2005. The Bantu Languages. *Bulletin of the School of Oriental and African Studies*, 68 (3). S0041977X05490278.

Lwanga-Lunyiigo, S. (1976). The Bantu Problem Reconsidered. *Current Anthropology,* 17(2), 282–286. http://www.jstor.org/stable/2741540

Madenge. 2021. *The Hadza Tribe: History, Culture, Religion, Myths.* United Republic of Tanzania. https://unitedrepublicoftanzania.com/the-people-of-tanzania/daily-life-in-tanzania-and-social-customs/major-tanzania-ethnic-groups/how-many-tanzania-tribes-biggest/the-hadza-tribe-history-culture-religion-myths-people-population-dna-baboon-hunting-gatherers-david-choe-women-culture-bushmen-hadzabe/#Hadza_Tribe_History

Maringozen. 2022. *Zwide KaLanga The Great King Of The Ndwandwes Who Created Mfecane Wars In The Southern Africa.* Opera News. https://za.opera.news/za/en/culture/50f210af883c2d7a432 a1f75837e4cba

Mbuti Pygmies. n.d. Anthropology Research. https://anthropology.iresearchnet.com/mbuti-pygmies

McCleland, D. 2019. *Port Elizabeth of Yore: The Khoi and San – The First Inhabitants.* The Casual Observer. http://thecasualobserver.co.za/port-elizabeth-yore-khoi-san-first-inhabitants

Mcginnis, B, C. 2017. *African Tribalism.* Penn State. https://sites.psu.edu/global/2017/04/19/african-tribalism

McKie, R. 2009. *How Neanderthals Met a Grisly Fate: Devoured by Humans.* The Guardian. https://www.theguardian.com/science/2009/may/17/neand erthals-cannibalism-anthropological-sciences-journal

Mpepereki, S. 2014. *Tracing the Shona Back to the Great Lakes Part 3.* The Patriot. https://www.thepatriot.co.zw/old_posts/tracing-the-shona-back-to-the-great-lakes-part-three

Mvenene, J. 2020. *A History of the abaThembu People from Earliest Times to 1920.* African Sun Media.

Ndlovu, R. 2021. *Venda People Culture and Language.* Buzz Feed. https://buzzsouthafrica.com/venda-people-culture-and-language-2

Nicolaides, A. 2011. *Early Portuguese imperialism: Using the Jesuits in the Mutapa Empire of Zimbabwe.* International Journal of Peace and Development Studies, 2(4), 132-137.

Nurse, G. (1973). Ndandwe and the Nguni. *The Society of Malawi Journal,* 26(1), 7–14. http://www.jstor.org/stable/29778286

Oluach, R. 2020.The *History of The Great Changamire Dombo.* Africa OTR. https://africaotr.com/the-history-of-the-great-changamire-dombo

Patou-Mathis, M. 2020. *The Origins of Violence*. Unesco. https://en.unesco.org/courier/2020-1/origins-violence

Pearce, D. G., Lewis-Williams, J. D., & Pearce, D. G. 2004. *San spirituality: roots, expression, and social consequences*. Rowman Altamira.

Peires, J. B. 1982. T*he house of Phalo: a history of the Xhosa people in the days of their independence*. Univ of California Press.

Penn, A. 2019. *Homo Sapiens and Neanderthals: Did They Mate? Battle? Both?*. Shortform. https://www.shortform.com/blog/homosapiens-and-neanderthals

Pontzer, H. 2012. *Overview of Hominin Evolution*. Knowledge project. https://www.nature.com/scitable/knowledge/library/overview-of-hominin-evolution-89010983

Power, C. 2015. Hadza gender rituals–epeme and maitoko– considered as counterparts. *Hunter Gatherer Research*, 1(3), 333-359.

Press News Agency. 2021. *What Drove Homo Erectus Out of Africa*. Press News Agency. https://pressnewsagency.org/what-drove-homo-erectus-out-of-africa/

Pygmies. n.d. Yaden Africa. http://www.yaden-africa.com/the-culture/tribes/pygmies

Pygmy peoples: Ethnic group of center africa. n.d. Native Breed. https://www.nativebreed.org/pygmy-peoples-ethnic-group-of-center-africa

Rigby, N. 1994. Tall tales, short stories: The fiction of Epeli Hau'ofa. *World Literature Today*, 68(1), 49-52.

Rimmer, L. n.d. Prehistoric Empires – The Geographic Ranges of 5 Human Species. Abroad in the Yard. https://www.abroadintheyard.com/prehistoric-empires-geographic-ranges-human-species

Rogers, K. n.d. *The expansion of the Bantu out of western Africa and the eradication of the indigenous peoples of central and southern Africa*. Doc Droid.

https://www.docdroid.net/Hc2nulc/bantu-expansion-eradication-pygmies-khiosan-pdf

San. n.d. Siyabonga Africa. https://www.krugerpark.co.za/africa_bushmen.html

Schoeman, S. 1987. *Settlement in South Africa: Early migrants and the Nguni. Africa Insight,* 17(3), 192-198.

Shangaan Tsonga. n.d. Kruger Park. https://www.krugerpark.co.za/africa_shangaan_tsonga.html

Smillie, s. 2019. *The Lost History of the Griqua.* New Frame. https://www.newframe.com/the-lost-history-of-the-griqua

Smith, A. 2020. *Interesting Things That are Most Recognized About the Culture of the Xhosa People.* Buzz South Africa. https://buzzsouthafrica.com/xhosa-people-tradition-and-dance

Stapleton, T. J. (2006). *Faku: rulership and colonialism in the Mpondo Kingdom (c. 1780-1867).* Wilfrid Laurier Univ. Press.

Story of the hare. n.d. Sacred Texts. https://sacred-texts.com/afr/xft/xft25.htm

Strynatka, c. 2017. *Religious Belief System of the Khoisans.* Class Room. https://classroom.synonym.com/hinduism-worship-of-the-sun-12087091.html

Swazi culture: The language, food and tradition of the Swati people. n.d. Answers Africa. https://answersafrica.com/swazi-culture-the-language-food-and-tradition-of-swati-people.html

The arrival of the Khoisan. 2020. SA History. https://www.sahistory.org.za/article/arrival-khoisan

The Batwa people. n.d. Bwinid Forest National Park. https://www.bwindiforestnationalpark.com/the-batwa-people.htm

The history of the San. n.d. Exploring Africa. https://www.exploring-africa.com/en/botswana/san-or-bushmen/history-san

The history of Vhavenda people. 2022. Opera News. https://za.opera.news/za/en/culture

The San. 2019. SA History. https://www.sahistory.org.za/article/san

Thembuland. n.d. SA History Online. https://www.sahistory.org.za/place/thembuland

Tietz, T. 2016. *The Dscovery of the Tuang* Child.Sci Hi Blog. http://scihi.org/discovery-taung-child/

Tsui-Goab. n.d. Tormento SA. http://tormentosa.co.za/Wiki/Topic.php/Spoiler/Tsui-Goab

Twice, N.P.K. 2021. *The True History of Nguni People.* NPK Twice. https://npktwice.wordpress.com/2021/08/18/the-true-history-of-nguni-people

Unkulunkulu. n.d. Gods of Creation. https://godsofcreation.weebly.com/unkulunkulu.html

Warten, W. 2019. *Amapondo:Mpondo People.* Blog Spot. https://mzansiyoutube.blogspot.com/2019/02/amampondo-mpondo-people.html

White, R. 2018. *When and Why Did Our Human Ancestors First Leave Africa?* UT News. https://news.utexas.edu/2018/07/11/when-and-why-did-our-human-ancestors-first-leave-africa/

Why do people form groups. 2020. Reference. https://www.reference.com/world-view/people-form-groups-8a80cb5051495940

Wilson, E, O. 2012. Biologist E.O. *Wilson on Why Humans, Like Ants, Need a Tribe.* News Week. https://www.newsweek.com/biologist-eo-wilson-why-humans-ants-need-tribe-64005

Written in the sand. n.d. Sassi. http://www.san.org.za/history.php

Xhosa. n.d. SA History Online. https://www.sahistory.org.za/article/xhosa

Yenhaka, M. n.d. *A History of the MutapaEmpire.* Tracks 4 Africa. https://media.tracks4africa.co.za/users/files/w314706_1651.pdf

Yong, E. 2016. *Humans: Unusually Murderous Mammals, Typically Murderous Primates.* The Atlantic. https://www.theatlantic.com/science/archive/2016/09/humans-are-unusually-violent-mammals-but-averagely-violent-primates/501935/

Zulu folktales. n.d. S Life. https://slife.org/zulu-folktales

Zulu. n.d. South African History Online. https://www.sahistory.org.za/article/zulu

OTHER BOOKS BY HISTORY BROUGHT ALIVE

- Ancient Egypt: Discover Fascinating History, Mythology, Gods, Goddesses, Pharaohs, Pyramids, and More from the Mysterious Ancient Egyptian Civilization.

Available now on Kindle, Paperback, Hardcover & Audio in all regions

- Greek Mythology: Explore The Timeless Tales Of Ancient Greece, The Myths, History & Legends of The Gods, Goddesses, Titans, Heroes, Monsters & More

Available now on Kindle, Paperback, Hardcover & Audio in all regions

- Mythology for Kids: Explore Timeless Tales, Characters, History, & Legendary Stories from Around the World. Norse, Celtic, Roman, Greek, Egypt & Many More

Available now on Kindle, Paperback, Hardcover & Audio in all regions

- Mythology of Mesopotamia: Fascinating Insights, Myths, Stories & History From The World's Most Ancient Civilization. Sumerian, Akkadian, Babylonian, Persian, Assyrian and More

Available now on Kindle, Paperback, Hardcover & Audio in all regions

- Norse Magic & Runes: A Guide To The Magic, Rituals, Spells & Meanings of Norse Magick, Mythology & Reading The Elder Futhark Runes

Available now on Kindle, Paperback, Hardcover & Audio in all regions

- Norse Mythology, Vikings, Magic & Runes: Stories, Legends & Timeless Tales From Norse & Viking Folklore + A Guide To The Rituals, Spells & Meanings of Norse Magick & The Elder Futhark Runes. (3 books in 1)

Available now on Kindle, Paperback, Hardcover & Audio in all regions

- Norse Mythology: Captivating Stories & Timeless Tales Of Norse Folklore. The Myths, Sagas & Legends of The Gods, Immortals, Magical Creatures, Vikings & More

Available now on Kindle, Paperback, Hardcover & Audio in all regions

- Norse Mythology for Kids: Legendary Stories, Quests & Timeless Tales from Norse Folklore. The Myths, Sagas & Epics of the Gods, Immortals, Magic Creatures, Vikings & More

Available now on Kindle, Paperback, Hardcover & Audio in all regions

- Roman Empire: Rise & The Fall. Explore The History, Mythology, Legends, Epic Battles & Lives Of The Emperors, Legions, Heroes, Gladiators & More

Available now on Kindle, Paperback, Hardcover & Audio in all regions

- The Vikings: Who Were The Vikings? Enter The Viking Age & Discover The Facts, Sagas, Norse Mythology, Legends, Battles & More

Available now on Kindle, Paperback, Hardcover & Audio in all regions

FREE BONUS FROM HBA: EBOOK BUNDLE

Greetings!

First of all, thank you for reading our books. As fellow passionate readers of History and Mythology, we aim to create the very best books for our readers.

Now, we invite you to join our VIP list. As a welcome gift, we offer the History & Mythology Ebook Bundle below for free. Plus you can be the first to receive new books and exclusives! Remember it's 100% free to join.

Simply scan the QR code to join.

Keep up to date with us on:

YouTube: History Brought Alive

Facebook: History Brought Alive

www.historybroughtalive.com

Made in the USA
Columbia, SC
09 December 2023